USING HYPNOTISM

G.H. Estabrooks

Dedicated to

DR. G. B. CUTTEN

Former President of Colgate University
and an American pioneer
in the field of hypnotism

PREFACE

SINCE the days of Count Mesmer, discoverer of "mesmerism", the name originally given to the strange condition
of the mind which we now call the hypnotic trance, this
mysterious force has been exploited and discredited by pretence,
preposterous claims and charlatanry.

The author believes that nothing but harm can come of allow-
ing such an important field of human experience to remain
shadowed by popular ignorance and suspicion. Genuine Hypnotism actually stands in the same category as chemistry,
physics or mathematics. It is based on definite basic laws and
principles which have been discovered by patient experiment
and research; and just as astronomy has evolved from the
superstitions of astrology, and chemistry from the medieval
search for the magical "philosopher's stone", so Hypnotism has
evolved from the "mesmerism" of the eighteenth and nineteenth centuries into a true science, a branch of the great subject of the human brain and human consciousness. The main
facts and rules on which the science of Hypnotism are based
are known to all competent students of the subject, just as the
general laws of chemistry are known to chemistry students; and
those general laws of Hypnotism are popularly presented in this
book.

There are, however, certain specific and highly technical applications of these rules which are unsuited for presentation in
detail in a popular book, and these the author has had to touch
on lightly, especially on the practical use of Hypnotism in modern warfare. The intelligent reader of Chapter 8, "Hypnotism
in Warfare", will sense that much more is withheld than has
been told, but as much has been revealed as is compatible with
public interest, or, in fact, as is possible under present circumstances.

CONTENTS

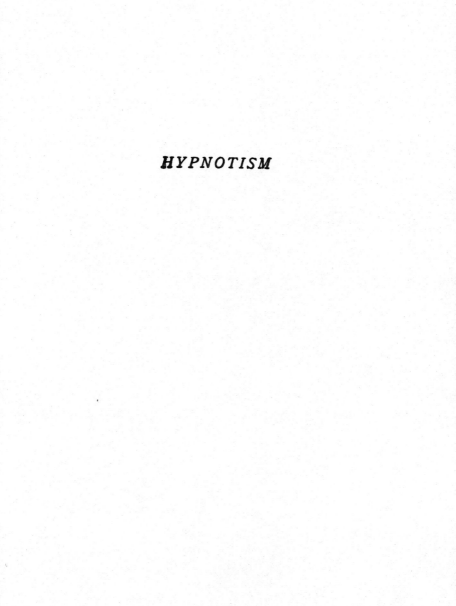

HYPNOTISM

Chapter I

THE INDUCTION OF HYPNOTISM

PERHAPS the best approach to an understanding of hypnotism is through the popular but somewhat unscientific idea of the unconscious mind. For example, we all have friends who walk in their sleep, in some cases performing feats of balancing on narrow balconies which would be impossible in the waking state. When they awaken, they have no knowledge of what has happened yet their bodies were certainly under control of some directing force.

Better as an illustration is the man who talks in his sleep. At times we can enter into conversation with him. If we are careful and know how to proceed, he will talk just as sanely and often far more frankly than when awake. Yet when we do awaken him, his mind is a blank as to what has occurred. Again, it would appear that something must be guiding his thoughts during this period of conversation. We will call this "something" the unconscious mind, a very convenient name for our own ignorance, and a concept we will have to examine much more carefully in later pages.

This last example provides us with an excellent introduction to our subject, for the individual who talks in his sleep and answers questions is really hypnotized. In fact, this is one recognized method of producing the trance, namely by changing normal sleep into hypnotic sleep. The skilled hypnotist can generally take the sleep-walker or sleep-talker and shift him directly over into deep hypnotism without either the knowledge or the consent of his subject.

Let us see what appears to happen in such a case. When we are in the normal waking condition, the conscious mind is running the body. We act, talk, and think as we please, although

13

such a statement implies "free will," a very controversial point which we will avoid in this book as of only theoretical interest. But in deep hypnotism this conscious mind of ours has been dethroned. Our actions are now under the will of the operator who controls our activities and deals directly with the so-called unconscious mind.

If he tells us there is a black dog standing by our chair, we will see the animal clearly and pet it. We will hear a symphony orchestra at his suggestion and describe the pieces being rendered. He may suggest we are Abraham Lincoln and we will give his *Gettysburg Address* or he may tell us that we have absolutely no feeling in our jaws, that the dentist is about to pull a tooth and we will feel no pain. He may even throw the whole thing into the future, saying that tomorrow at four P.M. no matter where we are, we will suddenly see a black dog at our side, will pet him and lead him home.

So the first concept we get of hypnotism is that curious picture of an unconscious mind controlled by the conscious mind of the operator. The subject will accept any suggestion the operator gives, within certain limits which we will consider in later pages.

In fact, suggestion appears to be the key of hypnotism. It is the method by which the hypnotist first gains his control and unseats the normal conscious mind. After this, he finds that his only way of controlling the subject is again through suggestion, for the subject left to himself will generally do nothing at all. He acts and behaves as if in normal sleep.

This unconscious mind is much nearer the surface in some people than in others. While the average reader thinks of hypnotism only in terms of the deepest stage or somnambulism, there are actually many degrees of the trance. Only one person in every five has the unconscious so accessible that the conscious can be completely unseated and the operator deal directly with the unconscious. Yet we find evidences of true hypnotic phenomena in almost everybody.

Let us follow the procedure of the operator as he induces hypnosis. This will serve to show all these various states and at the same time illustrate one method of inducing hypnosis, the method most in favor with the psychologist, who prefers the quiet of his laboratory to the stage of the "professional."

Suggestion is his key and relaxation makes the subject more open to suggestion. So, first of all, he has his subject seated comfortably in a chair or reclining on a couch. Then he "talks sleep." The subject is asked to close his eyes and the operator begins somewhat as follows.

"You are falling sound asleep. Relax all your muscles and imagine that you are going into a deep sleep. Deeper and deeper. You will not wake up until I tell you, then you will wake up quietly and you will always feel fine as a result of these suggestions. You are falling sound, sound asleep. Deeper and deeper, deeper and deeper." The hypnotist continues this formula for about five minutes and then tries the first and simplest test.

"Listen to me. Your eyelids are locked tightly together. Tight! Tight! Tight! Your eyelids are locked tightly together and you cannot open your eyes no matter how hard you may try. Your eyelids are locked tightly together and you cannot open them. You may try. I dare you!"

Then something very curious may happen. The subject is still wide "awake" in the sense that his conscious mind hears everything and remembers everything afterward. Yet for some reason or other he cannot get those eyes open, struggle as he will. He seems to forget which muscles to use, and raises his eyebrows in hopeless efforts to succeed. The operator is getting his first control over the unconscious and this control we can see progressing in definite steps. It is much easier, for example, to influence certain small muscle groups, say the eyes or the throat, than larger muscles as those in the arms or legs, while any attempt to get hallucinations—visions—at this stage would almost certainly fail.

We will find that, on this first trial, roughly one half of the subjects cannot open the eyes, while this percentage improves as we repeat attempts at hypnosis. In the long run, after, say a dozen trials, about ninety per cent of humanity will reach the stage when they cannot open their eyes.

The remaining ten per cent will generally report that they feel rested, relaxed, or sleepy, but will deny any real effects. Probably this feeling of relaxation and general sleepiness should be considered as one of the hypnotic phenomena at this very early stage, but it is hard to demonstrate, whereas eye-closure is quite definite.

However, we must note that whereas the hypnotist can get this closing of the eyes in ninety per cent of humanity, this does not necessarily mean that he can go any farther with his suggestions. He may and again he may not. That seems to depend almost entirely on the subject. There are many of these in whom it is easy to induce eye-closure, but quite impossible to get any tests which indicate a deeper stage of hypnotism. No matter how hard the hypnotist may try he can make no progress beyond this very elementary state and psychology is quite at a loss to explain why. Susceptibility to hypnosis seems to depend on certain personality traits which we do not know and cannot influence.

Should the hypnotist succeed in this first test with the eyes, he may proceed at once to one which indicates a somewhat deeper state, such as stiffening of the arm. He will end eye-closure and continue somewhat as follows.

"Now, relax everything. Relax your eye muscles. They are returning to normal. You are sound, sound asleep and will not awaken until I tell you. Then you will awaken quietly and easily. Relax everything. I am now about to make another test. Your right arm is becoming stiff and rigid at your side. Stiff and rigid. The muscles are tightening up. It is stiff and rigid as an iron bar. Stiff and rigid. You cannot bend your right arm. It is impossible to bend your right arm. You may try. I dare you."

Once again we may see that weird condition in which the patient is quite helpless to meet the challenge. He jerks the arm around with a curious sort of tremor and does his best, but his best produces no results. The arm remains stiff and rigid. Or he may meet the challenge quite successfully, relax his arm and open his eyes. In this case he has broken any influence we might have had. But even if he cannot bend his arm, this fact guarantees nothing as to his going deeper. As in the case of eye-closure, he may be wide awake and remember everything perfectly after the séance. The suggestions of the hypnotist have been successful up to this point. Beyond it he may be quite unable to make further progress.

If successful, another test is in order. Various operators will use different tests in different sequences but the idea is the same at this early stage, namely to involve larger and larger groups of muscles in these induced paralyses. The next move might easily be something like this. First of all we must remove the effects of the previous test. So we say:

"Relax, relax your right arm. It is returning to normal. Your right arm is resting quietly at your side and there is no strain whatsoever. You are sound, sound asleep. Deeper and deeper. Deeper and deeper. You are losing all control over your body. Your body is floating away and you can no longer control your muscles. For example, it is quite impossible for you to stand up. You are stuck in your chair and it is quite impossible for you to stand erect. You may try but you cannot. I dare you."

And the subject either does or he does not. He may pull himself together, even if the other tests have succeeded, open his eyes and stagger to his feet. On the other hand, he may make ineffective efforts to arise, then decide it is useless and relax in his chair.

In all these early stages of hypnotism we notice a curious lethargy, an unwillingness on the subject's part to exert himself. Very frequently, when we dare the subject to open his eyes, bend his arm or stand up, he makes no effort whatsoever. If we question him afterward, we find that he heard the challenge, was certain that he could move the muscles in question if he wished to, but he just couldn't be bothered to try. He was feeling quite comfortable and wished to remain so.

This must be listed as one of the earliest and best signs of success in inducing the hypnotic trance. It is a very significant cue which the experienced operator never overlooks, for it is not what one would expect if there were no influence. For example, suppose a hypnotist goes up to a gentleman sitting quietly in a hotel lobby and suddenly says:

"Mr. Smith. You cannot stand up. Your legs are paralyzed. No matter how hard you may try you cannot leave that chair." Mr. Smith, once he had recovered from his astonishment would probably stand up immediately and call the hotel management for protection against this madman.

But the hypnotic subject adopts an entirely different attitude. Not only does he think the operator's actions quite reasonable, but he makes no effort at all to assert his own independence. This curious lethargy, found in many people, generally indicates that the individual will become a good subject.

Should the operator be successful up to this point, he will proceed with the next step. He has demonstrated, to his satisfaction, that he can control the voluntary muscles, small and large, but this does not necessarily mean that he is dealing with a good subject, a somnambulist. He still has several steps to make. Next he will try automatic movements, talking to the subject somewhat as follows:

"You are sound, sound asleep, going deeper and deeper. Now, listen carefully. I am about to start your hands rotating one around the other. Here they go, round and round, faster and faster. Keep them moving. They are rotating faster and faster, faster and faster. You cannot stop them. No matter how hard you try, you cannot stop your hands from going around."

As in the previous tests we may get any one of three reactions. The subject may be able to resist the suggestion, stop his hands, and remain quiet. Or he may simply allow them to continue rotating, obviously making no effort to stop them. This is the type of reaction we mentioned in which the subject simply cannot be bothered to make the effort. Finally, he may try unsuccessfully to stop them, stiffening up the muscles in all sorts of curious ways, bumping his hands together, even gripping his coat in an unsuccessful effort to bring the movement to an end.

These automatic movements, as they are called, generally indicate a fairly deep stage of hypnotism. For some reason, they are much more difficult to obtain than mere paralysis or stiffening of any muscle or muscle group. When obtained they generally signify that the individual will be a very good subject, but this is not always the case. As before, many subjects will come to even this state of hypnosis and go no farther. The conscious mind refuses to relinquish its control and the subject will awake, quite aware of everything that has taken place.

This type of enforced activity can apply to any set of muscles, even those of speech. We can say to the subject, "Repeat after me the words 'Mary had a little lamb.' Now repeat it by yourself. Keep it up. You cannot stop it. You must keep repeating that sentence." And, in many cases, the subject will do as we have suggested.

If the operator has met with success up to this point, he will now suspect that he has a really good subject with which to deal and will try for somnambulism, the deepest form of the hypnotic trance. After he has convinced himself that the automatic movements are genuine or that the subject is too deep in hypnosis to even make the effort to resist, he may proceed somewhat as follows:

"Now I am going to ask you a few very simple questions. You are sound asleep and will answer me in your sleep, talking as you have heard many of your friends talk in their sleep. You will not wake up and will have no trouble at all in answering my questions." It is always well to repeat instructions several times so as to be sure that the subject understands.

Then the operator will ask some very simple questions, such as:

"Tell me, what is your home address?" "Where were you on your vacation last summer?" "How many brothers and sisters have you?"

Questions which have any emotional tone or which the subject may be unwilling to answer for any reason whatsoever should be carefully avoided at this early stage. The subject may easily awaken from this first light trance, have a vague memory of what has happened and refuse to have anything more to do with hypnotism. Even if he does not remember what has occurred, the unpleasantness of the situation may still hang over in a vague sort of way, and make it difficult to obtain full cooperation in the future.

Next, the operator may decide to have the subject stand up and walk around the room. This is accomplished by means of suggestion, which is the key to hypnotism. "You will now stand up. You will not wake up until I tell you, but will stand up, walking in your sleep as you have undoubtedly seen many sleep walkers. You will find no difficulty at all in using your muscles but will remain sound asleep. Now, stand up." And the operator helps the subject to his feet. Should the subject not wake up under this last test, we may be pretty sure that he is now in somnambulism, although a few subjects will cooperate very nicely up to this point but awaken when asked to move about. They may even walk around, obviously in hypnotism and still retain a fairly clear memory of what has happened after the séance is completed.

In general, we accept the hallucination as the final test of hypnotism. We can hallucinate any of the senses but the most common type is that of sight, the "vision." We proceed somewhat as follows:

"Listen carefully. When I give the word you will open your

yes but you will not wake up. You are still walking in your sleep. You will not wake up. You will see standing on the table in front of you a very friendly black cat. You will go over, pet the cat, then lift it up carefully and put it on the chair in which you have been seated." We repeat these instructions several times, then say, "Now open your eyes. Open your eyes. There is the cat."

This test is more or less crucial. The subject must be in deep somnambulism if he is to be subject to these hallucinations or visions. Should he not see the cat, then the shock of opening his eyes will probably awaken him completely and the séance is over. Should he really have a vision of the cat, his actions will be characteristic. He will pet the animal and play with it in so convincing a fashion that the operator need have no doubt as to what has really happened. The subject is in deep somnambulism and will remember nothing on awakening.

Actually there can be many a curious twist which will deceive even a trained hypnotist. The writer was demonstrating hypnotism before a group of medical students. The time was short, so it was agreed that he would take one of the men and simply go through the motions. The subject would cooperate and take the tests to the best of his ability, simply to provide a demonstration for the others of how hypnotism was produced.

We ran through the tests rapidly right up to hallucinations. Here the writer said to the subject, "Now open your eyes. There is an apple in my hand. Take it and eat it." The subject promptly opened his eyes, grinned, and said, "There's a worm in it." The operator took it for granted he was wide awake, asked him to sit down and continued his talk.

But when he dismissed the group, his demonstration subject remained seated, with his eyes wide open but unable to move. "Wake me up, will you," he said, "I can't move." So the operator waked him up in proper fashion. The operator must never take anything for granted in hypnotism, but must be quite certain that his subject is wide awake before leaving.

This is a very important point in technique. Let us suppose that the subject has arrived at somnambulism and the hypnotist wishes to end the séance. He awakens the subject by some such means as the following: "I will now count to five. By the time I get to five you will be wide awake and feeling fine. Wide awake and feeling fine. One, you are waking up; two, you are waking up; three, you are almost awake; four, you are nearly awake; five, you are awake."

Even if the subject should awaken by himself in any of the tests leading up to somnambulism, it is nevertheless a good plan, after he opens his eyes, to assure him, "All right, you're awake now. Wide awake and feeling fine." This very simple precaution may appear a little silly in many cases but it is always well to be sure.

We hear a great deal about the subject refusing to awaken from hypnotism. This appears to be a continual dread of people who are learning to hypnotize. What do they do if the subject will not awaken? If the operator will follow some such technique as we have outlined, this problem will never present itself. Throughout the entire séance we keep stressing the idea, "You will not wake up until you are told. Then you will awaken quietly and easily."

Should the patient refuse to awaken—the writer has never had such a case—the proper procedure is to allow him to remain quietly in the trance. The hypnotic "sleep" will change over to natural sleep and sooner or later the subject will awaken by himself. But experience will soon teach the operator that his real problem is to get his subject into hypnotism, not get him out of it.

That is the reason we insert the phrase, "You will not wake up until you are told." Some subjects have the habit, why we do not know, of suddenly opening their eyes in the very midst of the séance and awakening completely. They seem just as surprised as the operator, but undoubtedly there is some very good reason for this state of affairs. The following case is a good example.

The writer was hypnotizing a young man who gave all the signs of being an excellent subject. Everything went very nicely until the operator said, "I am now going to ask you a few simple questions which you will answer." Immediately, the subject was wide awake, trembling violently with every sign of intense fear. This was odd, so the operator repeated the séance with exactly the same result.

Then the explanation dawned on him. So the next time, before asking any questions, he said, "Listen carefully. There is nothing to fear. I am in no way interested in your private affairs. I wish to ask you a few very simple questions simply to show that you are in touch with me, that you are listening to me. If you do not wish to answer any particular question, just shake your head, but I assure you that I am not going to ask intentionally any question which could possibly embarrass you. Is that clear?"

He nodded his head and everything progressed in proper order from that point. Obviously it was the proverbial case of the guilty conscience. The subject feared the operator was going to pry into his secrets and awakened in order to protect himself.

The writer has described the hypnotic technique most used in the psychological laboratory but there are endless variations to this particular procedure, and several other entirely different techniques which are equally effective.

With this particular attack, for example, many operators prefer to start with the subject's eyes wide open, waiting until he closes them from natural fatigue. So far as the writer can see, it makes very little difference if we start with the eyes open or closed. He prefers to start with them closed.

Then the writer himself would not use the technique as he has outlined it. He awakens the subject after each test and starts all over again. A much slower approach, to be sure, but one which gives the operator ample opportunity to size up his subject and adopt his attack to any peculiarities the subject may have. We will see later that, on occasion, subjects do curious things which can be very disconcerting to an operator. The writer prefers his slower, more deliberate approach because it enables him to meet these peculiarities at the earliest possible moment. But most operators would consider him overcautious.

The writer also would never spend more than five minutes at any one séance in this early stage of the game, but he knows of excellent operators who will hammer right along for one hour if necessary in an effort to get somnambulism at the very first effort. And, of course, operators may vary the order of the tests and use different muscle groups. Speech muscles instead of eyes, inability to move a leg as opposed to an arm, or other substitutions.

But it all adds up to the same thing. If we use the "sleeping" technique the approach is slow, calm, and monotonous. The reader will note a complete absence of many things which popular opinion links with the hypnotist. We have described a procedure which anyone can master. There is no mention at all of "will power," for it has nothing to do with hypnotism. The operator does not dominate the weaker will of his subject and beat him into submission with his "dark, hypnotic eye." Quite the contrary. He does his best to persuade the subject to cooperate, making it quite clear that success is very difficult without this cooperation on the part of the individual in question. We will see later that a subject can very easily be hypnotized against his will but that this again has nothing to do with will power on the part of the operator.

We have not mentioned the famous hypnotic pass because this also is quite unnecessary, a hang-over from those early days of hypnotism during American Revolutionary times when Mesmer was passing his "magnetic fluid" into the bodies of his patients, and Benjamin Franklin with others in Paris was exposing Mesmer as a fraud.

Nor are there any special, intricate techniques which have to be mastered. Hypnotism has nothing of mystery in its nature. A small corner of science, it is open to all who are willing to use the necessary care in mastering a technique and persistence in applying the same.

In America we have been a little unfortunate in our introduction to hypnotism. Most of us have made its acquaintance via the stage and the "professional," whereas in Europe these public exhibitions of hypnotism are generally not allowed. As a result we find there in almost every town of any size some doctor who is an authority on the subject and uses it as needed in his practice.

But with us the medical profession fights shy of hypnotism, knowing full well that any individual who starts using hypnotism in his practice becomes associated in the public's mind with the stage artist, the quack. Even his companions in medicine look on him as a little queer, so that in America hypnotism has died a very natural death, so far as medicine is concerned. However, this very neglect on the part of the doctor has turned out for the best. It has forced hypnotism back into the psychological laboratory where the psychologist, with a much greater range of interest than his medical compatriot, has been doing some very excellent work during the past twenty years.

For the time being, however, this public prejudice is still very strong. The writer is especially anxious to present hypnotism to the reader as a branch of science quite divorced from mystery and from the supernatural. Certainly nothing we have presented in our technique for inducing hypnotism savors of the "black art" and we can assure the reader that the following pages will be just as free of any suggestion of the mystic.

There are many ways of producing the séance, so let us examine a technique at the opposite extreme from that we have described. The stage hypnotist breaks every condition which would seem to be necessary to the psychologist in his laboratory, but, strange to say, he is just as successful as is the true scientist. "The brighter the lights, the bigger the crowd, the better the success" as one professional put it. Obviously, then, quiet and relaxation are not necessary to the induction of hypnosis.

The following is fairly typical of the technique employed by the stage performer. He has the subject stand erect with his feet close together and proceeds somewhat as follows: "Stand erect and listen carefully to my voice. Close your eyes. Just imagine that you are a board standing on end. You are a board standing on end and you are falling back. You are falling backward into my arms. Falling back, back, back. Let yourself go. I will catch you. You are falling back, back, back. You are losing your balance and are falling backward." At this point the subject generally loses his balance and does fall backward.

The operator promptly stands him on his feet again and at once returns to the attack, this time standing in front of the subject. "Look into my eyes and clasp your hands together. Clasp your hands together firmly. Make an effort and put some muscle into those fingers. Clasp your hands together firmly, firmly. Your hands are locked together. Your hands are locked tightly together. You cannot take your hands apart no matter how hard you may try. Your hands are locked firmly together. I dare you. You cannot take your hands apart."

If he is dealing with a good subject the hands will be stuck together and it will be impossible for him to take them apart. So the hypnotist proceeds at once. "All right. Relax. You can take your hands apart. Keep looking in my eyes. Now open your mouth. Stiffen up your jaw muscles. Your jaws are stiff and locked in place. It is impossible for you to close your jaws. Absolutely impossible. You cannot pronounce your own name. Your jaws are locked in place and you cannot pronounce your own name. It is impossible for you to pronounce your own name. All right. Relax."

The hypnotist gives his subject no time to recover his poise, but returns to the attack at once. "Keep looking into my eyes. Stiffen out your right leg. Stiffen it out. Your right leg is stiff and rigid. You cannot move it. You cannot take even one step forward. Your right leg is stiff, rigid, and useless. You are rooted to the ground. You cannot move. All right, relax."

But the operator gives him no time to relax. Immediately he begins on his next move. "Close your eyes. The lids are locked tightly together. You cannot open your eyes. They are firmly closed. You are now falling backward into my arms. Let yourself go. You are falling back into my arms." The subject falls backward and the operator eases him down onto the floor or into a chair, and continues.

"You are asleep. Sound, sound asleep, just as if you have taken chloroform or ether. You are sound, sound asleep. Deeper and deeper. Deeper and deeper. You are sound, sound asleep." The operator continues in this vein for a minute or two, then at once shifts the subject over to active somnambulism.

"Stand up. You are sound asleep, walking in your sleep. Now open your eyes, but remain asleep. Look. There is an elephant standing over there. Here is a gun." He hands the subject a broom. "Now, go stalk the elephant. Remember he is a dangerous beast and you must take advantage of every bit of cover." Thereupon the subject proceeds to creep up on the supposed elephant, hiding behind chairs, tables or bits of scenery until he finally shoots the animal with a loud "bang" and proceeds to examine the corpse.

From this point the professional will probably go through the usual stage procedure, have his subject fish for whales in a goldfish jar, bark all around the stage on all fours, give a Fourth of July speech and finally awaken his very embarrassed subject just as he is about to remove most of his clothes. It is this sort of thing which has given hypnotism such a bad name with the average American, who always feels that somehow it is linked with sleight of hand and "magic" in general.

We may condemn the stage artist for bringing the subject into such disrepute, but we must admit that he gets results. The reader will also be impressed with the fact that his method of attack stands out in sharp contradiction to that previously described in almost every respect. Those conditions of quiet relaxation on which the psychologist insists are conspicuous by their absence. Nor is he in any way worried about having the cooperation of his victim. After the first half minute he runs things his own way, outraging the subject's dignity and good taste in every possible manner.

It is well to bear this stage technique in mind when we consider the real nature of hypnotism in Chapter III. Most psychologists are either unfamiliar with his technique or ignore it completely. If they numbered one or two of these professionals among their friends, they would not fall into some very common errors as to theory.

The stage operator will vary this technique indefinitely but his underlying theme is always the same. A high pressure attack which more or less aims at throwing the subject off balance. Then a rapid and continuous follow-up which does not give the subject time to recover himself. But we should note that, for all his extravagant claims, he ends with just the same proportion of somnambulists as does the psychologist; namely, one in five.

The two techniques we have described up to the present, with their endless variations, represent those most commonly used to induce hypnotism, but there are others. One, for example, simply aims at transforming natural sleep into the hypnotic variety. The method of procedure here is somewhat as follows:

The operator seats himself beside the sleeping subject and begins talking in a very low voice. "Listen to me. I am talking to you and you will answer in your sleep. You will talk to me in your sleep just as you have often heard others talk, but you will not wake up. You are sound asleep but you hear my voice clearly in your unconscious mind." The operator gradually raises his voice, puts his hand on the subject's head to further attract attention, and when his voice has risen to normal volume, say after five minutes, he asks the subject some very simple question, such as "Where do you live?"

In general, the operator has to press repeatedly for an answer until one of two things happen. Either the subject awakens, and this will occur in four-fifths of the cases or the subject starts talking in his sleep. When this occurs, the hypnotist proceeds as he would with any other somnambulist, has the subject stand up, walk around the room, open his eyes, see hallucinations and finally return to bed with the suggestion that he will sleep soundly until morning and awaken at the usual time. For obvious reasons, this technique is very limited in its possibilities for use, yet under certain conditions, as in a hospital, it does present very definite advantages.

At this point it would be well to mention the "disguised" technique. The reader will have noted that when the operator changes normal sleep into the hypnotic trance, the subject has nothing to say in the matter. This raises the interesting and very important question as to whether anyone can be hypnotized against his will and the answer is "certainly." If we wished, we could quibble as to whether transfer from sleep to trance was hypnotism "against the will" or only hypnotism "without the consent" of the subject. Not a very important point because the subject may definitely refuse to have anything to do with hypnosis in his waking state yet this sleep transfer method would still work. This, it seems, would be definitely against his will.

However, there are certain places in which hypnotism might be used where it would have to be employed without the consent of the hypnotized. Such would be the use of hypnotism in the detection of crime or in warfare. A prisoner in jail or after a battle certainly would not willingly coöperate with the hypnotist if he knew the operator was after information which might send him to the electric chair or which would put him in the light of a traitor to his country.

So here we employ the disguised technique. We hypnotize the subject without his realizing what is happening. We ask his cooperation in a harmless little psychological experiment using some piece of psychological apparatus as a front behind which to work. Perhaps the simplest is the device for measuring blood pressure. We explain to the subject that we wish to test his ability to relax, and we can measure this by his blood pressure. That sounds very reasonable so we fix the rubber band on his arm, tell him to close his eyes and relax all his muscles.

We further explain that, of course, the deepest form of relaxation is sleep, and that if the subject can fall asleep it will show that he has perfect control over his nervous system. Then we proceed to "talk sleep" much the same as in hypnotism, being careful to avoid any references to trances, séances or hypnotism, and omitting all tests except one. After five minutes, during which period we have checked several times on the blood pressure to keep up the delusion, we tell the subject that we would like to see if he can talk in his sleep, since this represents the very deepest form of relaxation. If he does, he is in deep hypnosis. If he does not, no one is any the wiser as to what has actually been taking place. We repeat this little experiment several times until we have obtained results or convinced ourselves that no results are to be obtained.

Should the authorities ever decide to use hypnotism extensively either in the detection of crime or in warfare, this disguised technique may prove extremely valuable. Not only is it just as effective as any other mode of attack, but it is of such a nature that very few laymen would recognize it as anything other than what it purports to be; namely, an experiment to measure ability at relaxation. Moreover, the apparatus used can vary indefinitely. The so-called lie detector provides an excellent screen behind which to work. The writer finds that an ordinary watch with which to take pulse rate as a measure of relaxation is quite as satisfactory.

The previous paragraphs also illustrate another very important point in any consideration of hypnotism. Science is eternally on the move, questioning, probing, inquiring. The truth of yesterday may be false today. Many of the older hypnotists, writing around 1900 were quite definite in their assertions that no one could be hypnotized against his will. They were just as sure that hypnotism could not be used for criminal purposes, and they were quite right, in so far as they knew hypnotism.

But these early authorities were almost always medical men. Their interest lay in treating the weaknesses of the human machine. To them such questions were merely side issues, and very unpleasant side issues at that. Hypnotism was unpopular, linked in the public's mind with black magic and mysticism. They felt it their duty to defend it at every turn. When faced with these very unpleasant possibilities they settled the issue with a few experiments which proved their own point, but which are quite worthless from the viewpoint of modern psychology.

The subject, armed with a rubber knife, would gladly murder his victim. Give him a steel knife, however, and he would recoil in horror. The subject could not be hypnotized when he made up his mind to resist, but was quite easily thrown into the trance when he cooperated with the operator.

We will see, in later pages, that all this proves very little. Hypnotism is now investigated in the laboratory by the scientist. He cares very little about the popularity of his subject and insists on a thorough investigation of every question. To be sure, the facts he unearths may be unpleasant. Hypnotism may be a very dangerous thing in the hands of the unscrupulous, but so is the aeroplane, the rifle, the disease germ. Science wishes to know the facts. Once discovered, these truths are handed over to the public. If that public uses the aeroplane to drop bombs, rather than to carry passengers, the scientist is in no way to blame. So with hypnotism. The psychologist seeks to unearth the truth. That is his problem. The use to which his discoveries may be put is something different again and something for which he has no responsibility.

Another most interesting way of inducing the trance is by means of the victrola record. The operator simply dictates his technique to the record, plays this back to the subject and the record will put the subject into hypnotism just as well as will the voice of the hypnotist. A very neat example of how little "will power," passes, and hypnotic eyes have to do with the trance. About as nonmystic a procedure as anyone could wish.

The writer prepared one of the first of these records with the assistance of the Victor people and it is now marketed through the Marietta Apparatus Company. Many others have since made their appearance, all good and generally intended for some specific purpose. It is now so very easy to record the human voice that there will undoubtedly be a great future for this technique. The operator will prepare a definite record for a particular subject, instruct him how to use it and literally apply absent treatment in the best sense of the word.

Yet we must bear in mind that this use of hypnotic records has very definite limitations. The record is excellent for purposes of instruction, which was the reason for its first appearance. It is very useful for experimental work, where the psychologist in his laboratory wishes to be sure that his subjects are receiving exactly the same instructions as are those in the laboratory of a colleague 1,000 miles away. It can even be used to induce hypnotism the very first time.

But the operator should always be present, for very naturally no record, no matter how skillfully devised, can meet the various emergencies which arise when we induce the trance. Some subjects tend to become hysterical, some even show a disposition to go into convulsions and some others are difficult to awaken. The victrola record cannot handle these situations.

However, there may be a real use for this technique after the subject has been hypnotized several times. Then it might be very useful from the medical angle, when the subject is being treated for, say, alcoholism or stammering. The doctor might very easily prepare a record for such a subject, aimed at reinforcing and repeating suggestions already given in the hypnotic trance. Such a record would, of course, be so arranged that it would also awaken the subject from the trance. This could very easily be arranged and would be a great convenience to both subject and doctor. Hypnotism is notoriously time consuming and any device which could meet this objection might make it far more acceptable to the average medical man. We will deal more fully with these proposals in a later chapter. There is always that very interesting possibility of hypnotism over the radio. While we do not have the slightest doubt that certain members of the radio audience could be thrown into the genuine trance by a hypnotist using such a means of contact, the whole thing is impractical. The operator is too far removed from his various subjects and should anything go amiss the chances for trouble, including lawsuits, would be infinite.

It is very possible that in future some enterprising company may devote a period to broadcasting health suggestions, which the audience will accept in the relaxed state and which might be very helpful. But this is only a possibility and something for the future. Up to the present nothing has been done. The proposal is open to many practical objections.

In future pages the writer will point out that we are often quibbling over words. Hitler was an excellent hypnotist, and we really mean that statement to be taken seriously. We will see that his technique was almost identical with that of the stage hypnotist, that the underlying psychology was the same and the results much more effective. To be sure, there were differences, but these differences were very superficial. So we do have hypnotism of a very effective type over the radio but it bears another label.

There has been a great deal of work done with drugs as an aid to hypnosis, all to practically no end. It would seem reasonable to the reader that any good anaesthetic, say ether, should make almost any person susceptible to hypnotism. The subject is "unconscious" in both states so what gives one should produce the other. Actually the subject is far from being unconscious, he is not "asleep" as so many people assume and all our work with drugs appears to have been wasted effort.

Perhaps drugs may still have a use in lowering resistance

to the trance. Some people are very susceptible to hypnosis but, for one reason or another, will not permit themselves to be hypnotized. In certain rare cases it may be advisable to hypnotize these people in spite of themselves. A light anaesthetic might cause them to lower their guard, so to speak, or to relax their antagonism. Then the operator might be able to induce the trance state. However, such a proposal is purely in the realm of theory. In so far as we are aware, there has been no extensive use of drugs along these lines.

The writer has also run across another curious proposal for the induction of hypnotism. We have all heard a great deal about jiu-jitsu, the famous Japanese technique of wrestling. It has been often reported that these experts were able to produce unconsciousness simply by pressure on a certain neck nerve. There seems to be no doubt of this and one of the writer's friends contacted a jiu-jitsu man so as to work with this lead. But apparently unconsciousness produced by such a means has nothing to do with the hypnotic trance. After all, there is no reason why it should, any more than any other form of unconsciousness such as that caused by the blow from a baseball bat or a boxing glove.

Still another intriguing possibility is the so-called animal hypnotism. We know that all animals from insects right up to apes can be "hypnotized," and this appears to hold for every individual animal of any given species. Man is an animal, so why not man? It would appear that this animal hypnotism, or catatonic immobility as it has been termed, has something to do with fear. The accepted way to hypnotize a sheep, for example, is to suddenly pull its legs out from under it, hold the animal firmly on the ground, then gradually relax the pressure. The animal will remain quiet for up to half a minute, then will recover with a jerk, shake itself and trot away. The same general technique applies to other animals.

But, unfortunately, the human, as is so often the case, stands in a class by himself. No one has yet discovered how to use the technique of animal hypnotism on man. He simply does not respond to these methods. And it really does not make very much difference, because psychology has now decided that animal hypnotism is something totally different from human hypnotism. We will see later that even the great Russian scientist, Pavlov, made the mistake of considering them identical as have many others, but our latest research would indicate they are quite different.

The scientist explores every possible lead. One of our foremost physicists discovered that if fish were placed in a magnetic field they would promptly become immobile, with the nose toward one pole, tail toward another. This looked like animal hypnotism and a possible technique for human hypnotism. But once again it did not work, this time because of the difficulties of making a suitable apparatus.

The successful hypnotist, like any other man of science must be somewhat of a fatalist. The laws of nature are not to be changed by any human ingenuity. In so far as the induction of hypnotism is concerned the law is one in five, at least in the present state of our knowledge. One out of every five subjects will, on the average, go into deep hypnosis or somnambulism and no operator, whatever his skill can better this average.

Nor does it seem to make very much difference who does the hypnotic work or what method he may choose to use. Needless to say, skill plays a large part in hypnotizing but granted an experienced operator results will be much the same. A good subject can be hypnotized by any operator using any method. We will see later that there are curious exceptions. Also that by using the post-hypnotic suggestion it is very simple to arrange matters so that the very best subject cannot be hypnotized by anyone with any technique. But our statement still stands as does also the statement that many individuals cannot be hypnotized by anyone, no matter how skillful the hypnotist or how hard the subject may try to co-operate.

Needless to say, it would be of great advantage if we could

discover beforehand who these very susceptible people are. The operator would then save himself much wasted effort. How does he do it? The answer is unfortunately all too definite. It cannot be done at least in the present stage of our work. We know of no tests which will foretell with any degree of accuracy which individuals will develop into really good subjects. Much work is being tried along these lines and some research is yielding promising results, as that at the Harvard Psychological Clinic. The fact remains, however, that we cannot as yet use any tests here with anything like certainty.

We can, however, save ourselves a great deal of work if we follow certain leads. In general, the individual who talks in his sleep will be a good subject. The person who walks in his sleep, the "natural" somnambulist, will almost always go into "artificial" somnambulism or deep hypnosis. The feeble-minded are notoriously hard to hypnotize, as are also some classes of the insane, as the schizophrenics. But the hysteric on the contrary is generally a very good subject. Children between the ages of seven and twelve are excellent, the proportion here running as high as four in five, as opposed to the one in five average of normal adults.

This leaves us with no means at all of judging the susceptibility of the average adult. But we can still do considerable to save ourselves time and trouble. We can use some of the simplest tests of hypnosis as indicators. For example, the "sway" technique helps us. Here we really borrow from the stage hypnotist. The subject is asked to stand erect and we attach to the top of his head a system of strings and wires which measure accurately the sway of his body. Then we ask him to close his eyes, suggest to him that he is falling backward and get an accurate measurement of just how far he does sway. The speed and extent to which he accepts these suggestions give us a fairly accurate picture as to his possibilities as a subject.

Another rapid way of picking the good subject, in the

absence of any equipment, is simply to use the test of clasping the hands, as mentioned previously. We begin by requesting the subject to clasp his hands firmly together, and to imagine as vividly as possible that they are locked together, that he cannot take them apart. We reinforce this by our own suggestions that the hands are locked tightly together and once again the difficulty he has in parting his hands gives us a fairly good cue as to what will happen with more advanced tests.

However, the writer finds that the best way to discover good subjects is by using group hypnotism. He takes a group of about a dozen individuals who wish to co-operate, seats them in chairs, tells them to close their eyes and proceeds to talk sleep. Then after a couple of minutes he dares them to open their eyes, and notes results. The entire group is told to awaken—just a precaution as almost never will anyone go into trance at such short notice—and next the operator asks them to clasp hands, following this by the usual challenge. Then he stiffens out the arms of the entire group and dares them to relax the arm muscles. Finally, he starts their hands rotating and defies them to stop the movement. After each test, of course, he assures himself that everyone is wide awake.

The experienced operator can easily pick the good subjects with such a technique, and have the whole thing over in ten minutes. He observes these individuals who are continually in difficulty when he challenges the group or who are too relaxed to even make an effort. These he notes as future good subjects and dismisses the group when he wishes. The only real difficulty here is one of discipline. The whole procedure is pretty certain to strike some member of the group as being very funny, but a little experience will soon enable the operator to handle these situations without offense to anyone.

A lazy man's way of handling this matter of group hypnosis when searching for subjects is to use the victrola record. The operator may either make one for himself or use one of those supplied by the houses which handle psychological apparatus.

It is very easy to get co-operation from a group with one of these records. It is impersonal and looks much more like a genuine psychological experiment, at least to the layman. Once again, with practice, it is a simple matter for the experienced hypnotist to watch the group and pick out the good subjects on the basis of how they behave to the victrola record.

Some people are so extremely susceptible to hypnotism that at times we get curious results even when using a victrola record. The writer recalls one such incident. He had a group who wished to listen to his record. They knew very little about hypnotism but had heard that this marvelous gadget, just on the market, would actually hypnotize.

They were all seated comfortably, the writer reached for the record—and it wasn't there. A colleague was using it in another building. So he took the first record in sight, put it on the victrola and said, humorously, "Now listen to that."

Returning five minutes later he was astonished to see that one of the group was evidently going into deep hypnosis. So he turned the record over and remarked, "That will do the trick very nicely." And it did. The subject was deeply hypnotized and had to be awakened by the usual method. The record in question was a Swiss yodelling song! The man expected to be hypnotized, was an excellent subject, and his own imagination did the rest.

The tests which we have suggested as of aid in detecting those individuals who will go into deep hypnotism, are, however, only bits of the hypnotic technique itself. As we mentioned before, there is no way of telling the good subject, except by actually using hypnotism in some form or other. Contrary to general opinion, susceptibility has nothing to do with a "weak will." Neither has it any relation to intelligence. In actual practice it is much better to deal with highly intelligent individuals. They will get the knack of the thing and co-operate more quickly than others.

Nor has hypnotism anything to do with the sex of the subject. Many people have the idea that women, especially young women, are much more easily put into the trance than are men. Scientific research gives no basis whatsoever for such an idea. There appears to be no difference.

We will mention here another point to which we will later return. Group hypnotism in the popular sense of the word is quite impossible. No hypnotist, no matter how good, could meet a group of, say, thirty people and hypnotize the lot, unless of course by some weird chance all thirty happened to be good subjects. The odds against such a chance are very heavy. In other words, the Hindu rope trick is not done by group hypnotism. As a matter of fact it never occurred at all in spite of a great deal of popular legend on the subject. If the reader doubts this statement, and he will, he may look up any good book on magic or any stage magician. We give some very good imitations in our modern theaters when the necessary apparatus is at hand, but this could never be duplicated in the open under the blazing Indian sun with the crowd surrounding the juggler on all sides.

The techniques we have described can be mastered by anyone, just as anyone can learn to run an automobile. To be sure, some people turn out to be much more expert drivers than others, but there is certainly no mystery connected with driving the auto. This does not mean that everyone should learn to use hypnotism or should, of necessity, be permitted to use it if he did learn. That is quite another thing. We simply say it is possible for anyone to learn and stress this point because of popular notions of will power, the dark hypnotic eye, black magic, and other weird ideas.

Finally, many readers may question the wisdom of being so very frank on this matter of inducing hypnotism. We reply that the danger is quite imaginary. The average layman cannot use hypnotism because he has neither the time nor the interest. A mastery of technique demands hard work, and the process of hypnotizing is notoriously boring and tedious. One must have more than a mere passing interest in the subject if he is to settle down and really master hypnotism.

In a later chapter we discuss the dangers of hypnotism, especially in connection with crime. Here, again, the point is largely imaginary, and the reader is asked to reserve judgment until we discuss such questions. The writer will contend that hypnotism can be used for criminal ends, but such use would demand an operator of the highest skill. For any amateur such attempts would only lead to prison. Moreover, our police are quite familiar with everything written in this book and could detect a crime involving hypnotism quite as readily as any other. This may come as a revelation to the reader but, for example, our own Federal Bureau of Investigation knows more about possible criminal uses of hypnotism than anyone in the country. So we may safely leave this aspect of our problem in the hands of the proper authorities, who are quite capable of handling it. The scientist is interested only in facts. How these facts will be used is a question which he is not called on to answer.

Chapter II

WE DEVOTED our first chapter to the induction of hypnosis, pointing out that only about one in five of the general population will go into the deepest stage of hypnotism; namely, somnambulism. We wish to deal here with the more common phenomena which we find in hypnotism once the trance has been induced.

The reader must bear in mind that, while the more striking things which happen are found only in the deepest stage, nevertheless there are many conditions in lighter states which are well worth our attention. We generally accept amnesia or lack of memory as the chief characteristic of somnambulism. The subject has no memory at all when he awakens as to what has occurred in the trance. Yet a great many things may occur with the subject wide awake.

For example, the writer had occasion to use hypnotism with a friend, a good pianist. He did not lose consciousness but it was quite possible to paralyze large groups of muscles, so much so that he was unable to arise from his chair. The operator asked him to open his eyes, moved the chair close to the piano and made a bet with him that he could not leave it for the next half hour. He played as well as ever, but every time he tried to stand up the operator simply said, "Sorry, it can't be done." That simple suggestion was quite enough to keep him glued in his chair.

This interference with use of the muscles is very easy, even in the light stages. Professor W. R. Wells of Syracuse University has made very extensive experiments with "waking hypnotism." This is a very interesting point since many of the older investigators thought hypnotism merely a special variety of sleep, a theory which is now generally rejected.

The writer recalls one of his very earliest contacts with hypnotism. A stage operator was demonstrating in the local theater. One of the audience, a dignified member of the community and a deacon in his church, turned out to be a very good subject. The hypnotist had him stand on his head, bark around the stage on all fours, take off a goodly portion of his clothes and give, in general, a very humiliating exhibition. He then awakened his subject who just as promptly knocked him down. The subject had been quite conscious throughout the whole performance but had been unable to resist the sugges- tions of the hypnotist. He remembered everything that had occurred and was very naturally indignant.

Wells produces his results in "waking" hypnotism with much the same attack as does the professional. A high pressure volley of suggestions is used without giving the subject time to re- cover his balance. With this particular technique he does not mention "sleep" and finds that the subject very often remembers everything when he comes out of the trance.

We also know that any good subject can recall consciously everything that has happened when hypnotized, if we assure him in the hypnotic trance that he will do so. As a matter of fact it is often quite enough for the hypnotist to say, in the waking state, "You will remember everything that occurred in the last trance. Think. It is all coming back quite clearly." The entire series of incidents will then return to consciousness.

But while unconsciousness may not be necessary to produce all the phenomena of hypnotism, the fact remains that the somnambulist generally remembers nothing unless we take some special steps to get recall. So we will describe the trance state from now on, using the typical somnambulist as an ex- ample.

The key to hypnotism is suggestion. The subject, left to himself, does nothing. The hypnotic state may then change to normal sleep and he will awaken in ordinary fashion, or he may just remain quiet, always open to suggestions from the operator but quite incapable of acting on his own accord.

This suggestion, by the way, need not be verbal, although that is the usual type. Any form of suggestion is quite satisfactory provided the subject understands what is desired. For example, if when the hypnotic trance is under way we take the subject's arm or hand and mold it into any gesture, then hold it there for a second or two the subject will conclude that we wish this sort of thing. No word need be spoken. With a little practice we will get "waxy plasticity" wherein the subject's limbs can be molded like wax into any position, no matter how uncomfortable, and will remain in the shape we have given them.

Moreover, the subject is very quick to co-operate with the operator and at times almost uncanny in his ability to figure out what the operator wishes. He seems to read his mind and this trait undoubtedly led many of the older hypnotists into wild conclusions as to the ability of the hypnotic subject as a "mind reader."

It is a very curious thing that the subject will only listen to the operator; he will receive suggestions from him alone. Others present may talk to him, shout orders and give suggestions, but he ignores them as completely as if they were on the planet Mars. This curious condition we refer to as "rapport." The subject, we say, is in rapport only with the hypnotist.

Here, we see one of those strange contradictions which are so characteristic of the hypnotized person for actually, he hears everything which is taking place, but for some curious reason he chooses to do a little acting. He behaves as if there were no others present in the room.

For example, we take a good subject and proceed to show how mind reading occurs. The operator conceals his handkerchief, tells the subject to concentrate and get the object in question. Others are present. They make suggestions and give him orders but he ignores them completely and is at a total loss to find the handkerchief.

Then, one of those present whispers to another, but quite loud enough for the subject to hear, "The handkerchief is in the brief case in the study." Apparently the subject has heard nothing but a minute later he goes to the study, opens the brief case and returns with the handkerchief. It can be shown by such experiments that rapport is not real. The subject always has his ears open to pick up any cue, yet in almost every case the new subject will immediately start on this little piece of fraud.

This illustrates a point we will mention frequently. The subject when hypnotized may be quite a different person from the same individual if awake. He is so anxious to co-operate, to show his abilities, that he may try almost any trick in order to do what the operator demands. This requires that in many tests we keep the subject under the very closest observation.

For example, the older hypnotists claimed many remarkable things about hypnotism. One of these was the ability of the subject to raise blisters under suggestion. The standard practice was to put a bandage on the subject's wrist and suggest to him very strongly that the bandage was a mustard plaster which would shortly produce a blister and strange to say, in many cases the suggestion was successful. An actual blister might not always appear but the skin under the bandage would become very inflamed and red, blood appearing in many cases.

Then some experimenters became suspicious. They left the subject in the room by himself but kept him under close scrutiny through a peep-hole. It was then found that the subject, in his great desire to co-operate, was playing tricks on the hypnotist. He would deliberately rub the bandage with all his strength so as to irritate the skin beneath. Worse still, some subjects were seen to take a needle, thrust it in under the bandage, and break the skin in this manner. Yet, when awake, these same subjects were models of honesty and even when questioned in hypnotism they would deny all knowledge of trickery. So we have to watch the subject very closely in many experiments. The mere fact that he claims to be in rapport only with the operator means nothing. It is just a little pose which, for some reason or other, he feels bound to maintain.

Another curious thing is that we can shift the rapport very easily. The operator merely says to the subject, "Listen carefully. Mr. Smith is here in the room with us. I am going to shift the control to Mr. Smith. He is standing in front of you. I will repeat the first five letters of the alphabet, a to e. When I get to e, Mr. Smith will be in charge. You will listen only to him and accept only his suggestions." Under these conditions Smith now becomes the operator and the subject will treat him as such until he chooses to hand back control to the original hypnotist.

So easy is this trick that we can even shift control from a victrola record to any operator who happens to be present. We simply work the suggestion into the victrola record, using exactly the same formula as given above. The operator then takes over control from the record, treats the subject as he would any somnambulist and awakens him whenever he chooses.

The mesmerist or magnetist of one hundred fifty years ago did even better. He would magnetize a tree. In future, the subject had only to touch the tree and he would go into the mesmeric trance, receiving all the beneficial effects of the magnetic fluid from the tree in question. Many of these old practices seem pretty weird but we must remember that science was then in its infancy.

Perhaps the best known of all hypnotic phenomena are the so-called hallucinations. The reader will be familiar with these if he has ever seen a stage demonstration of hypnotism. He will recall that the subject, following a suggestion by the hypnotist, will see an elephant or a tiger on the stage and will hunt it with a broom for a gun. The operator will put a goldfish bowl in front of him, tell him it is the Atlantic Ocean, equip him with a fishing line, and tell him to fish for whales. Actually this would be more in the nature of an illusion but they are so close to hallucinations that we will treat all under the same head. These hallucinations of sight or visions are very easy to get in any good subject and like everything else in hypnotism they depend on suggestion. The hypnotist simply tells the subject to open his eyes. Then he says, "Look. The door is opening and a black dog is coming into the room. His name is Rover. Go over and pet him." This he does. The hypnotist adds, "He's probably hungry. Better give him something to eat." The subject glances around, takes a plate from the table, puts a stick on it for a bone and proceeds to feed the dog. All this is done in a perfectly normal fashion which leaves very little doubt in the spectator's mind that the subject thinks he is dealing with a real dog.

The hypnotized person will treat every hallucination with great reality. Tell him the dog is friendly and he will pet it, but say the dog has bitten him and he may retreat in fear. Or he may seize the dog by the neck and throw it out the door; the type of reaction depends on how the subject would normally behave. Suggest to the subject that he is watching a football game and he will cheer on his favorite team in very convincing fashion. Tell him he is in a cathedral and he may kneel, that the police are coming in the front door to arrest him and he will try to leave by the back.

What we obtain depends largely on the type of individual. The writer has a favorite trick of telling the subject there is a "galywampus" in the room. Of course, neither the subject nor the operator has ever seen such an animal, so it is very interesting to note what will happen. Some subjects will simply look puzzled and refuse to answer. Others, realizing the joke, will grin and say, "There ain't no such animal" or pass it off with some such remark. But others will rise to the occasion in noble fashion. Recently one subject described it as "a pink elephant with wings, a trunk on both ends and bowlegged." Asked what noise it made, he replied, "That depends. When you mention

Roosevelt's name he laughs like a human but if it's Willkie he just looks sad and sighs." Needless to say the subject was a good Democrat, had a vivid imagination, and was using it.

The reaction to these hallucinations brings out a very important point which the reader must always bear in mind. The hypnotized person is still an individual, not a tool, and behaves according to his own background. Place a glass of water in front of the ardent prohibitionist, tell him it is whisky and he must drink it. Generally he will refuse. Insist and he may become very angry, even awaken from the trance. Place that same glass before another subject who has no such scruples and he will drink the liquor with great relish.

Tell a communist he is talking to a political meeting and that he is to defend capitalism. He will probably do just the opposite, criticizing his audience and their views in no uncertain fashion. The subject is always willing to play a part, provided it does not go against any deep-seated convictions. But when we suggest an act which is in conflict with any of these, he may become very obstinate. We will discuss this in a later chapter devoted to hypnotism and crime.

It is quite easy to hallucinate any of the senses, but not always quite as spectacular as in the case of vision. Hearing, for example, lends itself very easily to this attack. We can have the subject listen in rapt attention to a supposed symphony concert, describing every number and criticizing the way in which each is played. It is possible to have him listen to a political talk and then describe it afterward, for example one by Mr. Roosevelt. The experience will be very real and he will stoutly defend his views at a later period; this in spite of the fact that the President was on the air at exactly the time when he was supposed to be listening and gave quite a different address. After all, the subject contends he heard it and certainly believes his own ears!

In some of the senses we can obtain a curious mixture of hallucination, illusion, and anaesthesia. For example, take the following cases. It is quite possible to give the subject a glass of kerosene, tell him it is very fine wine, and have him drink it. He does so with great satisfaction. Or we can reverse the process. We can give him a glass of whisky, tell him it tastes vile and that he will be very sick to his stomach once he drinks it. That probably will also work.

Such a technique was once in great favor for treating alcoholics. If the subject proved to be a somnambulist, he was assured in hypnotism that every time he took a drink in future he would be violently sick. If it worked, and it generally would, the cure became an endurance contest with everything in favor of the hypnotist. After all, drinking is not much of a pleasure if every drink is only the prelude to a vomiting fit. G. B. Cutten in his *Psychology of Alcoholism* deals in detail with this matter of treating the drunkard.

Similarly it was once common practice to handle smoking by the same method. The subject was assured that tobacco smoke would in future taste very bad and a cigarette would be followed by an upset stomach. This was really hallucinating the senses of smell and taste. A friend of the writer in a near-by city tried this on a young man at the request of his parents but unfortunately he did not ask the consent of the subject beforehand. Once his victim heard of the plan he was very indignant over the whole thing, swore he would smoke in spite of any hypnotist and went at it again. In six months time he was smoking with reasonable comfort, but he almost ruined his digestion in the process.

Smell lends itself very nicely to hallucinations, one of our best tests of hypnotism coming in this field. If we have any doubt as to whether the subject is deeply hypnotized, we tell him he is about to smell some very fine perfume. We then hold a bottle of strong ammonia under his nose and tell him to sniff; if he is in deep hypnotism he seems to enjoy the perfume, but if not, or if he should be bluffing he will come out of the trance in very short order.

We also have some very curious cases wherein we can deceive

the skin senses. For example, we can take a pencil, hold it near the subject's hand, and tell him it is a red hot poker. If we touch the hand, he will draw it away, sometimes shrieking with pain. Actually, we have never been able to prove that the skin is really "burned" by this technique, although some of the older authorities did report just this. Proof in science, as we will later see, is no simple matter.

Since we are on the skin, let us report a very interesting experiment by Liebeault, the real father of modern hypnotism. He had one exceptionally good subject on whom he reported the following. He was able to trace letters on this man's forearm with the blunt end of a pencil. Later these letters would appear as letters in blood! Not only that, but with this one subject he carried the experiment even farther. The subject was able to do it himself, suggesting to himself—autosuggestion— that the blood letters would appear! Liebeault stresses the fact that such remarkable phenomena could only be obtained with the very best of subjects.

Liebeault did his work around the 1870's and no other operator since has been able to get these results. This tends to cast a doubt on the experiment since Liebeault may not have been careful enough with his subject. It is quite possible that, if left alone, he could have scratched his arm with a needle along the lines of the letters and yet, strange as it may sound, there is no reason why these results could not have been obtained. They would depend on the action of the autonomic nervous system and we do know quite definitely that we can influence this by means of hypnotism.

We really have two nervous systems in our bodies. All our voluntary muscles are controlled by the central nervous system, composed of the brain and spinal cord, but our internal organs also do their work by muscular action, in many cases. The lungs, heart, stomach, even the arteries and veins could never function if it were not for the activity of muscles and these "involuntary" muscles are under control of the autonomic nervous system. This system lies outside the spine and, although joined to it, acts in general quite independently of the other system.

For example, try and influence your heart beat as you read this book. It is almost impossible. Yet strange to say, we can influence the heart through hypnotism. We can make it beat faster by mere suggestion, especially if we tell the subject he has, say, just escaped from a bear and is very much excited. Excitement, as we all know, tends to make the heart beat faster and the scene we suggest to the subject is so real to him that he behaves as if it were a real bear. Yet very few of the readers could imagine such a scene vividly enough to get any real reaction. The writer once saw a stage hypnotist suggest to a subject that he was falling over a cliff. He was actually falling from a table onto a pile of cushions. The subject gave a wild shriek of fear as he fell and collapsed. *That* was genuine. A doctor and heart stimulants were necessary to save his life.

Nor could any of my readers by imagining that they were eating some very disgusting dish, make themselves vomit. Here again the hypnotist can influence the autonomic nervous system, as seen in the action of the stomach. As we mentioned before, we have only to suggest to the somnambulist that liquor tastes bad, that it is disgusting and in future he may find that even the smell of liquor will turn him sick to his stomach. Not only that, but we can influence the subject's stomach in much more subtle fashion. We can, for example, suggest to him that he is eating a beef steak. Not only will his mouth water but we will find that his stomach secretes the proper juices to handle the meal in question. For a very sane and critical discussion of all these rather unusual phenomena we refer the reader to the work by Clark L. Hull of Yale University, *Hypnosis and Suggestibility.*

A Russian psychologist recently reported an even more interesting stomach experiment. He claims that in hypnosis he was able to give his subjects large quantities of alcohol, with the suggestion that they would not get drunk. And they did not either in hypnosis or after the trance! We may add that before such claims could be accepted they would have to be checked on by many other operators.

At this point a very natural question will occur to the reader. Why all this doubt and uncertainty? If we are in doubt, then why not clear the matter up at once and in short order. Unfortunately hypnotism of all subjects does not lend itself to this offhand treatment. For example, let us take the question of muscular strength in hypnosis. N. C. Nicholson investigated this using the ergograph, an instrument designed to measure the amount of work a subject can perform with one of his fingers. It is easy to measure the work of a finger and what applies to the finger should, in theory, apply to any other group of muscles. Nicholson conducted a series of experiments and concluded that "during the hypnotic sleep the capacity for work seemed practically endless."

But later P. C. Young repeated Nicholson's experiments and found, at least to his satisfaction, that muscular strength in hypnotism was no greater than in the normal waking state. The results would have been far less disturbing had either of these men been poorly trained and incompetent. Unfortunately, Nicholson did his work at Johns Hopkins and Young did his at Harvard. Both were very careful experimenters. The sharp contradiction is hard to explain but, in the writer's opinion, was undoubtedly due to the attitude of the hypnotists. The good subject co-operates in wonderful fashion. Nicholson's subjects realized they were supposed to show an increase in muscular strength and did so. The opposite applied to Young's experiments.

A great deal of our work in hypnotism must always be carried out with this fact in mind for the subject tends to give what is expected. Returning to this matter of physical strength, we are all familiar, at least have read about, the uncanny ability of most subjects to rest with the head on one chair and feet on another. Then to have someone sit on their chest while they recite poetry. This muscular rigidity can be obtained in most good subjects, provided the hypnotist makes it quite clear that he expects it.

But if the subject suspects that the hypnotist does not want this result, he will not stiffen up his muscles. For example, we take a very good subject and tell him that we are now going to give him a very severe physical test, we are going to put his feet on one chair, his head on another, and sit on his chest. Then we say to someone present, "Of course, it's impossible. All this talk about seeing it done on the stage is nonsense. They use fake subjects and magician's tricks with which to do it."

Now we try to stiffen out our subject, but he knows we do not expect results. So we get none. He makes no effort and sags down in discouraging fashion whenever we try to stretch him between the two chairs. Yet we must bear in mind that there is no reason why we could not get this exceptional increase in strength. Few readers realize the tremendous strength of the human muscles, when we can really make them exert themselves. We use a drug named metrazol to treat a form of insanity, dementia praecox. This throws the patient into violent convulsions, so violent, in fact that he often breaks his own bones by the sheer force of muscular contraction. This is no wild myth but a grim fact of which every psychiatrist is very conscious.

A recent survey has shown with the aid of X-ray pictures that twenty-five per cent of all patients undergoing metrazol treatment actually crack some bones of the spinal column in these savage convulsions. The psychiatrist now uses another drug, curare, to offset this. Curare paralyzes the muscles, so they hope that the patient can now get the mental shock without the body strain. At the present writing we have not enough material to say that this treatment is as good as straight metrazol, which gives excellent results in many cases. But these examples, and we could give many more, will show the reader the tremendous power of the human muscles under certain conditions. So there is no reason why we might not get a great increase in strength with hypnosis.

Then there is another possible explanation. Fatigue is a defense to the body. When we feel tired it is a sign that we have worked hard enough and should stop until the body gets the waste cleared away from the muscles. There seems to be a fatigue center in the brain. If we can paralyze this, the individual will not feel tired, no matter how fatigued. We will see later that with hypnotism we can get anaesthesia or lack of feeling in many parts of the body. It may be that this great muscular strength in many cases is due to the inability to feel fatigue once the operator assures the subject that he can do great feats of strength without being tired.

This is one reason why no sane hypnotist would dare suggest to a football player before a game that he was to play the game of his life and would be able to put forth his very best without feeling in any way tired. Perhaps he would, but in so doing he might easily exert himself so much that he would die of a heart attack.

Returning now to this matter of producing blisters in hypnotism. Even if they were produced, it would illustrate nothing supernatural. The walls of the blood vessels are under control of the autonomic nervous system. We can definitely influence this system in hypnotism, but not in the waking state. Granted a person with a very sensitive skin there is no reason why these vessels could not break and let out blood or blood plasma under the bandage, so creating a blister or actual bleeding. Normally it will not occur so we tend to think of it as impossible just as we tend to feel that the subject cannot really increase his muscular strength. But, in the opinion of the writer, there is strong probability that blisters can be produced. He also feels certain that muscular strength can be greatly increased by means of suggestion.

We must again remind the reader that proof in science is often difficult to obtain, and in hypnotism this is notoriously so. There can be no doubt as to hallucinations and no doubt that we can influence the activity of most body organs. But we must suspend judgment on bodily strength and such curios as raising blisters; yet there are many other things claimed of hypnotism, some accepted and some in doubt.

Accepted, for example, is the fact that we can produce anaesthesia, loss of sensation in almost every sense organ. This is most easily seen in the loss of pain, technically known as analgesia. As a matter of fact, this was one chief use of hypnotism in the early days. An English doctor in India by the name of Esdaile performed the first such operation of which we have record in 1845. During the course of his long practice in that country he did thousands of operations, about three hundred of these being of a major character. Unfortunately or fortunately as the case may be, the use of chloroform was discovered about this time and ether shortly afterward. These drugs are far more certain in their effects and much easier to use than hypnotism, which rapidly vanished from use as an anaesthetic.

We do still hear of cases wherein it is used, in which the condition of the patient is such as to make the use of drugs inadvisable. There has also been some use of hypnotism in both Germany and Austria of late years, especially at childbirth. But the interesting fact is that hypnotism does banish pain. In fact, this absence of pain supplies us with our very best test of hypnotism in those situations wherein it is absolutely necessary to be sure that the subject is not bluffing.

The writer uses a little device known as a variac. This plugs into an ordinary light socket and delivers the exact voltage required. The contacts are placed on the palm and back of the left hand, blotting paper soaked in a saturated salt solution being used to insure the very best form of contact. Under these circumstances the reader would find fifteen volts very painful, twenty unbearable. But a subject in somnambulism can take sixty, even one hundred twenty volts without flinching.

Here we get into the usual argument so dear to the hearts of all psychologists. Is it anaesthesia or amnesia? Perhaps the subject actually felt the pain, but merely forgot about it on awakening, just as he tends to forget everything else which happens in somnambulism. The question is mostly of theoretical interest, but it serves to illustrate the difficulty of answering many a query in hypnotism. Considerable work has been done on this problem but up to the present the question remains unanswered. The anaesthesia may or may not be real but the subject acts as if it were, insisting after the trance that he felt no pain.

Yet, whether real or genuine, it does not have nearly as much importance as the average reader may think. Pain is the doctor's friend, although we as sufferers may not always see this point. It is nature's great alarm signal. Without doubt hypnotism could completely remove the pain in many a case of acute appendicitis, but that would not prevent the appendix from rupturing. It might only serve to lull us into a false sense of security. Similarly pain may mean many things. Gastric ulcer, kidney disease, rheumatism or an ulcerated tooth. The doctor's problem is not to remove the pain but the cause of the pain.

For example, two of the worst "killers" in the whole disease world are tuberculosis and cancer, mainly because they give us the warning after it is too late. Tuberculosis can be quite easily cured in its early stages, but unfortunately it is a painless disease. We can easily be suffering from an advanced case of tuberculosis and yet be fairly comfortable, beyond a very troublesome cough and a feeling of continual fatigue.

Likewise most cases of cancer could be cured in the early stages, if only medicine could locate them. But cancer also uses a painless attack until the disease is well advanced. When we finally go to our doctor with severe abdominal pains and he diagnoses it as cancer, we might as well call the undertaker the next day and get our earthly affairs in order. The reader is very liable to become much too enthusiastic over the possible uses of hypnotism. It undoubtedly has it uses, and we will deal with these in future pages, but the obvious use is often more apparent than real.

We can render any of the sense organs anaesthetic. Pain gives us our most graphic results but vision is just as easily influenced. We can suggest to the subject in hypnotism that he is blind and to all outward appearance he becomes so. With his eyes wide open he will walk into a chair or make no movement at all when someone pretends to strike him in the face.

Is this blindness genuine or is the subject again staging a little act for the benefit of those present? Very probably it is a bona fide performance. The subject is really blind, but only in a functional sense. It might be well to explain what we mean by this statement, by way of helping us to understand the problem.

We divide human ailments into two broad groups, the functional and the structural or organic. For example, our hospitals for mental disease always contain a large group of insane suffering from dementia praecox, or schizophrenia. This is a functional insanity as there seems to be nothing wrong with the brain. If we examine it after death we find it is just as good as our own. On the other hand, we could also find in any such place a number of cases with general paresis, generalized syphilis of the brain. These people are also "crazy." Very much so in fact, and here we would find that the brain had been severely damaged by the syphilis germ.

Thus with insanity, for instance, we have both the functional and structural cases, both equally insane but in the former the brain is uninjured, in the structural cases the brain has been harmed by something, be it syphilis, sleeping sickness, tumor, stroke, or what not.

The blindness we get in hypnotism is of the functional type. There is nothing whatsoever wrong with the eyes, yet it is very real for all that. This sounds hazy and mysterious so let us see how a man could be stone blind with eyes and brain just as good as our own. In order to see, hear, feel pain, or experience any sensation at all the action of nervous tissue must be involved. Here the unit is the neuron, the separate tiny telegraph line which nature binds together in the bundles we call nerves.

But these neurons have some very interesting qualities which make them much better than our own human made wires. The most interesting point about the neuron, from our point of view, is its ability to break contact. Nervous tissue is, of course, all over the body but the brain and spinal cord are the chief centers of concentration. Especially in the brain do we have a tremendously complex telegraph exchange.

Literally billions of these tiny wires connect with each other. We call the point of contact a synapse, and here very fine brush-like structures from one neuron come very close to those from another so that the "spark" can easily jump the gap. As we learn anything, from running a typewriter to Chinese, pathways are worn through the "grey matter," so that the passage of the nerve current over certain synapses becomes much more easy.

But the reverse of this can also happen. When we "forget" it is a sign that for some reason or other the pathway we wish to use has become blocked, probably because the little brushes which make contact at the synapses have drawn so far apart that the current cannot pass. It seems probable that in sleep all intercommunication in the grey matter is cut off in this way. Similarly when a person gets "drunk" or is knocked unconscious by a blow on the head. We could also quote experiments from various drugs, such as arsenic, to uphold this view.

Now let us suppose that the operator suggests to his subject in hypnotism that his whole right arm is senseless, has no feeling in it. If the synapses open in those parts of the brain where we feel pain from that arm, then the nerve currents simply cannot register. We have cut off communication just as effectively as if we cut the nerve leading from the arm, yet there is nothing wrong with the brain. Structurally, it is perfect, all the parts are there and capable of working. But they are not working or "functioning" because of this break at the synapses, so we say that we have a "functional" anaesthesia in the arm. And this "opening" of the synapses is probably due here to suggestion.

This anaesthesia is very real, for all that. No amount of play acting would enable any subject to lie quietly on the operating table and have his arm amputated. Yet this can be done in deep hypnotism. Similarly we can get the functional blindness we have been discussing. In this case it is very difficult to prove that the subject is not bluffing. We have no easy, positive tests, but we can argue from the analogy of anaesthesia in the arm. This is very real, so anaesthesia in vision is probably just as real. And, of course, there is no "structural" injury to the brain.

The trouble with this very neat synaptic theory is that it is almost impossible of proof, though it seems highly probable. We can see the synapse under the microscope, but we cannot see its movement because this only takes place in living tissue and would be difficult to get under the very best conditions. We cannot turn a microscope on the brain of a living animal.

Yet some day we may be able to actually observe these movements in the synapses. Several years ago Spidell of the University of Virginia won the highest award from the American Association for the Advancement of Science by demonstrating a very beautiful technique. He was actually able to see the growth of nerves in the tail of a living tadpole! That may strike the reader as very unimportant but science values curious things. A year or two previous to this another man got this award by showing that protozoa in the intestines of the termite digested his wood diet for him and so allowed him to live on pure wood! That solved many a problem that had puzzled the zoologist. Only a year or two ago a psychologist, Maier, won the coveted award by demonstrating that he could drive rats insane by frustration, by continually puzzling them over the location of their food. Silly? That experiment means a great deal to the psychiatrist, the "nerve specialist," who treats the human insane.

So with luck in the near future we may actually be able to see the movement at the synapses through the microscope. At present it is a very neat theory, probably true but incapable of being proven. Yet it shows us how all these curious things may happen in hypnotism and be very real, yet involve no change or injury to the brain. When the psychologist or doctor mentions that word "functional" he is not merely throwing up a smoke screen to hide his ignorance. Functional blindness is a very real thing as thousands of "shell shock" cases from the war can testify.

Similarly by means of hypnotism we can obtain functional deafness or anaesthesia of the ear, the organ of hearing. It seems to be very real for the subject is quite unconcerned with even the loudest of noises. He simply ignores them. A little more spectacular is anaesthesia of smell. We have already mentioned the fact that in deep hypnosis the subject can inhale strong ammonia without a quiver. If we suggest it is perfume, he even enjoys the process and that involves hallucination.

Taste is equally easy to reach, for the subject will chew up and swallow the vilest tasting dishes we can give him if we assure him that he tastes nothing, or even better, if we tell him he is eating a beef steak. All these weird things have a sound physiological basis. If the reader would really understand hypnotism he must banish from his mind all trash about the mystic and the supernatural. Everything is to be explained and can be explained by the activity of a very complex nervous system. With hypnotism we can cut out entire memories for certain events which have taken place in past years. The surgeon can do the same up to certain limits, but he must injure the nerve centers permanently. We can make the shift with no injury and at far greater speed than any telephone exchange.

We have considered the matter of anaesthesia of the various senses. How about hyperesthesia? We heard a great deal about this in days past, about the ability of the subject to develop great keenness of vision, to smell the very faintest odors or hear the very smallest sounds. Let us take a typical experiment as reported by Bergson, a French philosopher much interested in hypnotism.

He had one very excellent subject, a boy, with whom he could get the most unusual phenomena. Bergson was very much interested in the matter of telepathy or thought transference, and with this boy he proved it to his satisfaction. The subject would stand up facing the hypnotist who would then hold an open book behind the subject's head. The operator would thus be able to see what was on the pages but the subject, of course, could not, unless he had eyes in the back of his head.

Bergson was then delighted to find that the hypnotized boy could read the printed pages which only the operator could see. He had proved telepathy, which was a great achievement. Or had he? Bergson was a very careful investigator. He became suspicious, for the thing worked too well. Then he made an astonishing discovery. The boy was not reading his mind at all but the reflection of the book in the hypnotist's eyes! The letters on the reflected page would have been about 1/256 of an inch high; in other words, microscopic. Moreover, having once discovered the trick, Bergson had this subject demonstrate with other things, such as photographs reduced to very tiny dimensions. There was no doubt about it. This particular subject in hypnotism had a keenness of vision which was equal to that of a microscope.

Unfortunately, as so often happens when we consider the work of these older authorities, there is the usual joker. No one has been able to repeat Bergson's experiment, and proof in science is essentially a matter of repetition. It is very difficult to say why this experiment cannot be repeated. Certainly no one would wish to accuse Bergson of deliberate fraud. Very probably he was not careful enough with his controls; he did not watch his subject closely. At any rate, all that modern science can do is reserve judgment and hope that some operator will be able to duplicate his results under proper conditions.

Those of us who are familiar with the older type of hypnotism know of another experiment which bears on this subject of visual acuity. The operator would take, say, twenty perfectly blank white calling cards and tell the subject that he was about to show him some photographs. Then, as he placed these blank cards before the subject he would stop at one and say, "Look. There is a photograph of your mother. Do you recognize it?"

"Certainly."

"Will you recognize it again?"

"Of course."

The operator made a slight mark on the back of this card so that he would be able to pick it out again. Then he continued to show the rest of the pack.

Next he shuffled the cards, handed them to the subject and said, "Now pick me out your mother's photograph." Strange to say, the subject could do so! The writer has been able to demonstrate this himself and has seen it done by others.

Apparently what actually happens is something like this. The subject realizes that he is supposed to remember that particular card so he looks at the face very carefully and remembers some very trifling difference in the edge of the card, picks out some flaw in its surface or some trifling difference in texture. When next he looks over the cards he choses his mother's "photograph" by the card which he thus remembers.

This would not, perhaps, be so much due to greater intensity of vision as intense concentration and an ability to remember some very tiny detail. This is not as farfetched as it may sound. Those of the readers who have had the pleasure (?) of knowing the professional gambler and the opportunity of studying his cards realize with what speed and accuracy he can spot his "marked" cards while dealing hands to four or five at once. There is at least one concern in the United States which specializes in the manufacture of such marked decks, the "marking" consisting of some very slight variation in the pattern on the backs of certain key cards. If the average human in his normal state can arrive at such perfection through practice, there is no reason why the hypnotic subject, with his great powers of concentration could not do the same.

We have another very interesting type of experiment quoted by the older writers. This involved the sense of smell. They would take the handkerchiefs of a dozen people, allow the subject to smell each one, then mix them up in one mass and ask the subject to return them to their owner's. And the subject would oblige! But unfortunately there was far too great a chance of the subject picking out the handkerchief by other cues, as the make of the article, or expression on the owner's face to allow us to accept these old experiments at their face value.

At present the verdict of psychology on hyperesthesia is "unproved." As a matter of fact very little careful work has been done on this subject in the laboratory. Almost the only good piece of investigation here was by P. C. Young at Harvard and he says that the senses of the subject in hypnotism are no more acute than they are in the normal state. We must simply wait for more work. The writer feels that hyperesthesia probably does exist, that Young's negative results were due to the attitude of the operator, so very important in all this work. But neither can the writer prove his point.

It might be well here to explain just why we have all this trouble about proving a point. Proof in science, especially in psychology, is no easy matter. First, the individual case may mean very little, although even one subject who could demonstrate his ability consistently could do a lot. But in general we must have a group of subjects and this group must be "statistically significant," so that the results cannot be charged to chance. Such a group, to be above criticism should number at least seventy!

Then we must have a control group, who have not been hypnotized with which to compare the experimental group.

This should be just as large, same sex, and as near as possible the same age, education, and economic status. This control group in a subject like hypnotism is very important because even if we could show that a group in the trance did have very great keenness of the senses, we leave ourselves wide open to criticism. How do we know they could not do the same in the waking state? Try and find out? Not at all, because we might be running into the results of posthypnotic suggestions given without intention on the part of the operator, something we will discuss in the next chapter.

All these precautions may appear nonsense to the average reader but science is a very stern taskmaster. Any psychologist who runs experiments on too small a group, or on a group which is not checked against a properly selected control group may prepare for some very rough sledding. Needless to say, the task of preparing seventy somnambulists is a very difficult one. Then we have all the problems of keeping strict observation during the experiment. So the reader must remember that we do not settle these problems overnight with a couple of subjects or by the comfortable "arm chair philosopher" method. There is probably no more difficult branch of research in all science, so please be lenient when we continually say that such and such results are still in doubt.

There can be no doubt, however, about delusions, or false beliefs. Do not confuse these with illusions or false sense impressions, so closely related to hallucinations. For example, if we place a black hat on the table, and say to the subject, "Look. There is a black cat," he will pick up the hat and caress it as he would a cat. It is a false sense impression. But if we say to him, "You are now a dog. Get down on all fours and bark. There is another dog there in the corner. Chase him from the room," he will give a ludicrous imitation of a dog. This is a false belief, although seeing the other dog was an hallucination—neat little points about which it is very easy to become tangled.

These delusions, as we will see later, may be of the very

greatest importance, especially when we consider the possible tie up between hypnotism and crime in a later chapter. For example, suppose we say to the subject in hypnotism, "You are Mayor La Guardia of New York City. I want you to give a political speech." He will do his best to imitate the fiery Mayor and may give an astonishingly good speech. He believes himself to be the Mayor, a delusion or false belief.

Now we go a step further and say, "You were in Utica this afternoon between four and six o'clock. You visited the station and while there you saw Mayor La Guardia pass through the station on his way to the Hotel Utica. You will maintain this when you wake up." When he awakens, he will stoutly insist against all argument that he was in Utica and did see the Mayor, telling how he got there, how he got back and weaving a story which at least sounds convincing.

Suppose we go a step further. "You saw the Mayor pass through the station. Then you went into the taproom. There you overheard two men at the next table discussing a plot to assassinate the mayor this evening as he boarded the train for New York City. Here are the pictures of the two men. Be sure you remember them for you will see them again tonight at the Utica station." Once again a delusion, mixed with hallucinations and the posthypnotic suggestion, but primarily a delusion, a false belief, yet one which might make things very bad for two innocent men in Utica.

These delusions can be extremely real and the subject will defend them even when they are quite impossible. We say to a subject, "You were in the first World War with the Americans. You then went under the name of Captain G. N. Smith. Remember this when you wake up." When he awakens we bring up the subject of the last World War. He volunteers the information that he served in it under the name of Captain G. N. Smith. You point out that he is only twenty five. He would have to be at least forty five if his story were true. He maintains he really is forty five and then the battle is on. We attack him on all sides, pointing out how ridiculous his claim is. He defends himself with a beautiful series of lies and finally becomes quite indignant when we continue to doubt his word. Of course, here again we run into the problem of whether he is just bluffing, playing a part to please the hypnotist or really does believe he was Captain Smith in the last war—a very difficult point to decide.

So also are those curious cases which we call "regression" and which we can get in hypnosis. For example, we take a subject of forty years old and say to him, "You are now a boy of five. You will behave and think exactly as you did at the age of five." He gives a very convincing demonstration. We then say, "Now you are ten. Grow up to that age." He does so. Next we have him progress to fifteen.

Is it genuine? It certainly looks like a good case of faking. But strange to say, if we try him out with the intelligence test we find that he hits the proper mental age and intelligence quotient with very considerable accuracy. Of course, he could also fake this but it is very doubtful if any of the readers, unfamiliar with intelligence tests, could give the proper answers for a child of five, ten, or fifteen. It really looks like genuine regression which we know does take place in actual life. Much more work must be done on this subject, most up to the present being in Russia and perhaps not too carefully supervised.

We hear much in some literature about the ability which subjects have to reckon time in hypnosis. We can tell them that they will be able to tell exactly when 4453 minutes have passed and they will call the time exactly. Once again, not proved to the satisfaction of science. For example, one of the older experimenters, Bramwell, working around 1895 found that one particular subject could actually call the time to the exact minute.

But unfortunately he had no control subjects. What guarantee do we have that this subject or any of the readers could not do the same thing in the normal waking state? Ridiculous! Not at all! Try it on yourself. When you are lying quiet and relaxed, note how very steady is the heart beat. If it is sixty eight to the minute it will not vary more than one or two strokes in an hour. It is a simple matter of counting. If the subject is allowed to awaken, the very strictest watch would have to be kept that he was not counting the ticks on a clock, listening to the town clock or actually consulting his own watch.

In the psychological laboratory, at least up to the present time, we find no evidence of such capacity. Stalnaker and Richardson have done the best work here and their results show no increase in ability along these lines. Another example of why we must be very critical of the work by the older authorities. The writer always suspects that in these laboratory experiments the operator has the wrong attitude. He is out to "debunk" hypnotism, the subject realizes this, and helps in the de-bunking process with all his ability. We have considerable evidence for this in some experiments but only time and much work will tell how important operator-attitude may be.

It is very easy to make serious mistakes in hypnotism. The writer has made at least one he knew of, possibly many more. We use in psychology a very neat little piece of apparatus to measure the "psycho-galvanic reflex." This measures the resistence of the body to a very small current of electricity, the resistance generally being taken through the hand. It is a very curious thing that this resistance changes under any emotional strain. Suppose it is normally 5,000 ohms. The experimenter pricks the subject with a pin. Immediately the resistance drops to 4,000 ohms, swinging back again to 5,000 after about half a minute.

Equally interesting is the curious behavior of skin resistance in sleep. It will normally go to 40,000 or 50,000 ohms. The writer found in a series of experiments that the skin resistance of a subject when hypnotized also soared to 50,000 ohms. This proved conclusively that hypnotism and sleep were closely associated. The writer publishes his results—and they were found to be completely misleading. They were good as far as they went, only they did not go far enough. Other experimenters demonstrated that while this was true for hypnotism induced by the "sleeping" method, it was true only for this method and only as long as the subject remained quiet. The moment he got up and walked around his resistance became that of the normal waking subject.

Now, of course, the writer should have taken all this into consideration before publishing results, but man is just mere man. Science progresses by such mistakes. One research worker finds the subject will commit a crime in hypnosis. Another goes out to prove him wrong—and does so to his satisfaction. Then the fat is in the fire until one backs down or the consensus of scientific opinion proves him wrong. The writer has backed down at least once, may do so many more times, so it ill becomes him to criticize others too severely. The reader must realize that his opinions on some points as expressed in later chapters of this book are only his opinions. He is convinced that the weight of scientific evidence is on his side, but hypnotism, of all subjects, does not lend itself to dogmatism. We must await very extensive research before we have the final answer to many problems.

Clairvoyance, the ability to see distant scenes, is one such example. Many of the older authorities were quite positive that their subjects could describe events hundreds of miles away, say in the old home town. The writer has often met amateur operators who would proudly show how a subject could tell just what was taking place in some town of Tennessee or Kansas. But they never took the trouble to check up! F. W. H. Myers in his *Human Personality and its Survival of Bodily Death* seems to have felt that in hypnotism the psychic or supernatural powers of some subjects could be increased.

But modern psychology brings in another verdict of "unproved," in this case very highly improbable that it ever can be proved. The reader should get a clear distinction in his mind.

For example, there is not a reputable psychologist in the United States who would dare write an article questioning the existence of hypnotism and certain phenomena in hypnotism. His reputation would be ruined.

With reference to spiritism, and psychic research, the exact opposite is true. No one would dare say that clairvoyance or mind reading, as two examples of such phenomena, were proved. Some, such as J. B. Rhine at Duke University might say they believed in the existence of telepathy, even had a certain amount of evidence in its favor, but proof? That is something quite different again. A blunt assertion that the matter was settled to the satisfaction of psychology would find ninety-nine per cent of the psychologists registering an emphatic "no." This applies to all so-called spiritistic phenomena.

We further note that recent work by the group at Duke University interested in extra-sensory perception shows that hypnotism has nothing whatsoever to do with the abilities of people along these super-normal lines. So the reader will realize that hypnotism has no relation to spiritism or the supernatural. In later pages we will use hypnotism as a means by which to explain the trance state of the medium. Also such phenomena as automatic writing, crystal gazing, automatic speech, even talking with the dead. But even so we shall see that the things we find are quite normal, quite within the limits of what might be expected in the teachings of psychology.

The reader who is familiar with hypnotism cannot have failed to note that we have not mentioned several of the more interesting phenomena. For example, the famous posthypnotic suggestion and also autosuggestion. These are so very important that we cannot treat them in this short space, so we devote the next chapter to their consideration.

Then there is that very interesting question of dissociation, considered by some the key phenomenon of hypnotism. We prefer to deal with this problem in our chapter, *The Nature of Hypnotism,* since it is so closely linked with the entire theory of hypnosis.

Also we have avoided mentioning one of the most useful of all hypnotic phenomena, at least from the viewpoint of medicine. This is that curious ability which the somnambulist has to recall long forgotten childhood memories. This is the keynote of "hypno-analysis," a branch of psychotherapy which is destined to assume more and more importance as the prejudice to hypnotism in this country diminishes.

Associated with this is hypermnesia, wherein the subject in hypnotism or as a result of posthypnotic suggestion is supposed to develop a much better memory for things which have occurred in the immediate past, such as the learning of poetry or of history. This we postpone until we consider the possible uses of hypnotism in education.

Then we might mention other curiosities of the trance which we leave to later chapters, such as the ability to form conditioned reflexes and persistence of normal reflexes, all important but best reserved to our chapter on theory.

Will the subject in hypnotism commit a criminal act? Even more interesting, will he confess to crime in the trance state? Obviously these questions involve some very important phenomena of hypnotism. Just as obviously these questions cannot be answered in a few pages so we devote a later chapter to this whole question of the connection between hypnotism and crime.

Here we have only presented the more spectacular side of hypnotism, things which can—or cannot—be demonstrated in five minutes with any good subject. Far more important to psychology are the questions of hypnotism in education, in crime, even its possible uses in war. These, we will see, can only be investigated by very long and careful work. Some, indeed, cannot even be studied properly in our present day society. The solution must wait for the future. But the past few pages cover most of those things which the lawman associates with the word hypnotism. We now pass on to the more unusual phenomena concerning which the average reader probably knows very little.

Chapter III

THERE is a rule in hypnotism that everything we get in the trance can also be obtained by means of the posthypnotic suggestion. Also, that anything we find in either can be found in autosuggestion; and, finally, that everything we obtain in any of the three will be encountered in everyday life. In this latter case we refer to the subject as hysteric, neurotic, or even insane and will leave the consideration of these everyday cases to a later chapter on mental disease.

Let us take a typical posthypnotic suggestion. The operator says to the subject in somnambulism, "Now listen carefully. After you wake up, I will show you the ace of spades from a pack of cards. When I do this, you will see a black dog come in through the door. He is a very friendly dog, so you will pet him, then you will give him a bone. He belongs to Professor Fowler so, after you have fed him, you will call Fowler on the telephone and ask him to come get the dog." The operator repeats these instructions and asks the subject if he understands them thoroughly. Then the subject is awakened.

Five minutes later the hypnotist picks up a deck of cards, selects the ace of spades, and lays it on the table in front of the subject. The latter seems wide awake in every sense of the word. He glances at the door and says, "Why, here is Fowler's dog. He looks hungry. Come on in, fellow, and have a bone."

He pats the phantom dog, takes a plate from the table, puts on it an imaginary bone, and continues to fondle the dog as he eats it. Then he suddenly says, "You know, I don't believe Fowler knows where that dog is. I think I'll call him on the telephone and let him know."

So he goes to the phone and puts through his call, all the time talking in a perfectly normal manner about his garden, his auto or any other topic of conversation in which he may have been engaged. Fowler, who knows what is happening, comes over for a cup of tea. All the time he is in the room the subject keeps playing with the dog and finally says good day to the professor and his phantom pet in quite normal fashion.

Such is the typical picture of a posthypnotic suggestion. Some subjects act in a dazed condition while carrying out such orders but this is easily corrected by the suggestion that they will be wide awake and perfectly normal during the whole procedure.

Let us examine this type of suggestion more closely, for as we will see later it explains a great deal in abnormal psychology. It is a curious thing that the subject does not have to be in the deepest trance or in somnambulism to get the posthypnotic suggestion. To be sure it is much better if we start off from the deep state, but not absolutely necessary. We say to a subject in hypnotism, "After you awaken, I will tap three times on the table with my pencil. You will then have an irresistible impulse to take off your right shoe." Then we awaken him and find out that he remembers everything. Nevertheless we tap three times on the table and at once there is clear evidence of an inner conflict. He wants to take off that shoe but has made up his mind he will not. Like one possessed of a devil, he runs his hands through his hair, shakes his head, gets up and walks around the room muttering to himself, "I won't. I won't do it."

Finally the strain becomes too great and he says, "Oh! All right, then. Have it your own way." He takes off the shoe and sits down looking vastly relieved. While we can get this reaction in some subjects who do not enter somnambulism, in general they can fight off the suggestion. They still show evidence of a desire to carry out the order, but will sit still, grit their teeth, smile triumphantly and say, "No." And in most of these cases "no" means "no."

At this point, we should mention a very necessary precaution which should be taken in all this work. The subject must never leave the room until the suggestion has been removed. There are two ways of doing this. Re-hypnotize the subject and remove the suggestion, or, far easier, have him carry it out with his own consent. Simply say, "Very well. That test failed but I want to make sure that we have no trouble with it in the future. Take off your shoe and put in on again, just to clear the wires."

A doctor friend reports a very interesting case which happened to him twenty years ago. A patient came complaining that he was being followed by a big, black dog. The patient knew quite well that there was no dog around, but for all that he could not escape from the delusion that this dog was always at his heels. The doctor worked with him for a week with no success. Then the patient himself gave the answer. A stage hypnotist had been in town. He had volunteered as a subject, went into deep trance and remembered nothing of what happened until he was awakened at the end of the show. But the next day this dog delusion started and had been with him ever since.

The doctor found the answer in short order. Inquiring among his friends he found that the subject, the night of the show, had kept the house entertained by running around the stage for half an hour always pursued by a big, black dog. He was one of several subjects and this was his "stunt." He was hypnotized at once, the posthypnotic suggestion removed, and, after a couple of séances, had finally got rid of his phantom friend.

One of the real dangers of hypnotism lies right here. We may easily instill in the subject's mind some conflict, without in any way intending the same. One of our best operators reports the following case. The subject, in deep trance, was told to drink a glass of whisky. He was a prohibitionist, had never tasted liquor and refused. But the day after the trance, he told the hypnotist that, for some unknown reason, he had developed a crazy idea of entering every saloon he passed and having a glass of whisky. The operator said nothing, re-hypnotized the subject and this time took care that he removed all posthypnotic suggestions.

The best procedure is as follows. After each trance, if any posthypnotic suggestions have been given, explain to the subject in the waking state just what has occurred. Then assure him that the suggestion in question has now been completely removed. If he has any hint of its still persisting, he is to look up the operator at once. With experience the hypnotist will never have any trouble along these lines but he must always realize that he must exercise great care.

There are two outstanding facts about these posthypnotic suggestions which link them very closely to the so-called Freudian "complex." First, these suggestions, as do those in hypnosis proper, have a very curious compulsive force. When given to a subject in somnambulism they simply "must" be carried out. The writer recalls one very interesting example while doing graduate work at Harvard. Professor William McDougall was always greatly interested in hypnotism. Under his leadership some very valuable research work was always under way.

On one occasion a group was gathered in his office. One of these graduate students was an excellent hypnotic subject and the professor hypnotized him. Before awakening the subject, McDougall said, "When I light my cigarette, you will take the ace of spades from the pack of cards on the table and hand it to me." Then he awakened the subject and later lit his cigarette.

Now it happened that this particular subject was greatly interested in hypnotism and quite familiar with its use. He at once reached over for the pack of cards, then suddenly stopped.

"Do you know," he said, "I believe that is a posthypnotic suggestion."

"Very probably," McDougall replied, "what do you want to do?"

"I want to give you the ace of spades."

"That's right. It is a posthypnotic suggestion. What are you going to do about it?"

"I won't do it."

"I bet you fifty cents you will."

"Taken."

Then came a very neat demonstration of this compulsive power of the suggestion. The subject was obviously in difficulties. Extremely restless, he would keep drifting toward that pack of cards, then pull himself together, and sit down only to be on his feet again in a minute's time wandering around the room in a most unhappy fashion. But he did resist and at the end of an hour and a half he collected his fifty cents, wiped his brow, and left the room.

But his troubles had only started. McDougall had purposely omitted removing the suggestion. The subject had a great deal of work to do but simply could not settle down. He was haunted by the ace of spades. Finally at four o'clock in the afternoon he gave up the struggle, returned to the building, had the janitor let him into the office, got the ace of spades, looked up the hypnotist at his home, and handed it over plus a one dollar bill.

These compulsions arising from the posthypnotic suggestion work in very curious ways. For example, we say to a subject, "When you awaken I will reach for a cigarette. You will then hand me the ash try from the mantelpiece." When he is wide awake the operator reaches for his cigarette and the subject promptly hands him the ash tray.

"Why did you hand me that tray?"

The subject looks puzzled. "Well, why not? You are smoking and have no ash tray."

"It was a posthypnotic suggestion. See if you can pick out the next one and resist it."

We try again. This time we say, "When I stand up to leave the room you will hand me a coat. By accident, however, you will hand me Mr. Jones' coat, the one with the velvet collar."

This time when we stand up, he immediately hands us Jones' coat, then notices his mistake and apologizes profusely. We say, "Fooled again! Another posthypnotic suggestion. See if you can catch us."

In hypnotism we then say, "When you awaken we will mention the shipping losses caused by the submarines. You will then reach for the *New York Times* and quote us the losses for the last four weeks."

He is awakened. Five minutes later the hypnotist mentions shipping losses. He promptly reaches for the *Times* and just as promptly stops.

"No, you don't. Not this time. That is a posthypnotic suggestion. I won't carry it out."

"How do you know it is a posthypnotic suggestion?"

"I just feel it in my bones. Sort of an urge to do it and a very uncomfortable feeling when I resist. That feeling would never come from anything else."

"I bet you can't resist it."

"Yes, I can. Much as I want to get my hands on that *Times*, the thing is not irresistible."

"Very well. Look up the figures any how just to ease your mind."

This subject, highly intelligent and himself a psychologist, could pick out the curious drive to carry out the suggestion and so was able to identify it. The reader will note a point which is very important for later discussion. The subject tends to carry out these suggestions without any hesitation, especially when they fit into the social situation in which he finds himself. However, immediately he finds out the cause of his actions, he just as quickly decides to resist. Whether this resistance will be effective depends on many factors, especially the depth of the trance and the attitude of the hypnotist.

Sidis in his *Psychology of Suggestion* brings out the importance of operator attitude very clearly. He quotes from his very wide experience to show that the subject will resist a suggestion if he has the least idea that the operator does not fully expect him to comply. On the other hand, if the hypnotist makes his suggestions in a firm voice which does not express the slightest doubt as to their acceptance the order will be obeyed.

Science here tends to lean over backward in its effort to become scientific and in doing so becomes very unscientific. We cannot adopt completely the methods of the physical sciences, such as chemistry. The attitude of the experimenter matters nothing here. If he adds zinc to sulphuric acid, the result is quite clear cut and definite, whatever may be his attitude. But in suggestion this attitude is tremendously significant. A suggestion given in a voice which does not express conviction is not nearly as potent as one given with determination and force.

We do not have to experiment with hypnotism to see the truth of this statement. Any effective public speaker knows that confidence, conviction, and force are necessary to sway his audience. We will later see that a Hitler uses all the techniques of a stage hypnotist and uses them with excellent results.

So we must always bear in mind that, while psychology claims to be a science and to follow the scientific method, this personal factor introduces an element which is quite foreign to chemistry, physics or geology. The psychologist, in his determination to get standard conditions, may, in some cases, completely defeat his own ends and become a very unscientific scientist. Hypnotism supplies us with our most glaring examples and, for this reason, hypnotism is probably the most difficult of all subjects in psychology to investigate. The personality of the operator is of such great importance.

The reader must bear this constantly in mind when, in later pages, we discuss such subjects as the possible use of hypnotism for criminal ends and for the detection of crime. Here we will see that some of our very best men, such as M. H. Erickson at Eloise State Hospital, are emphatic that hypnotism cannot be used in either situation. But we will also see that others of equal reputation, as W. R. Wells of Syracuse University or L. W. Rowland of University of Tulsa, are just as emphatic that it can. This presents a very confusing picture to the average reader and tends to discredit this branch of psychology. Actually such results must be expected until we find some way of evaluating the personal factors of both the hypnotist and the subject.

There is a second characteristic of the posthypnotic suggestion which is of the very greatest importance. This we term rationalization. The subject tends to rationalize, to find excuses for his actions and, strange to say, while these excuses may be utterly false, the subject tends to believe them.

For example, the writer says to a very good somnambulist, "After you awaken I will sit down by the piano. You will then go to the bookshelves, select the third book from the left hand side, second row from the top, turn to page 127 and read the first paragraph." The subject remembers nothing of what the operator has said, yet, when he seats himself by the piano, the subject wanders over to the library, selects the proper book, opens to page 127 and starts reading. It happens to be a textbook on biology.

The operator interrupts. "Why are you reading that stuff to me?"

"Well, yesterday I had an argument with Professor Smith about the action of the chromosomes in reduction-division, and I thought you could help me out."

The subject was a medical student, the story fitted together neatly, and he evidently believed it—only it was quite untrue. He had not seen Professor Smith for a week and had had no argument about the action of the chromosomes. This case is typical. The subject always finds an excuse to justify his conduct, and this conduct may be pretty hard to justify, as in the following case.

The operator hypnotizes a subject and tells him that when

the cuckoo clock strikes he will walk up to Mr. White, put a lamp shade on his head, kneel on the floor in front of him and "cuckoo" three times. Mr. White was not the type on whom one played practical jokes, in fact, he was a morose, non-humorous sort of individual who would fit very badly in such a picture. Yet, when the cuckoo clock struck, the subject carried out the suggestion to the letter.

"What in the world are you doing?" he was asked.

"Well, I'll tell you. It sounds queer but it's just a little experiment in psychology. I've been reading on the psychology of humor and I thought I'd see how you folks reacted to a joke that was in very bad taste. Please pardon me, Mr. White, no offence intended whatsoever," and the subject sat down without the slightest realization of having acted under posthypnotic compulsion.

Next came a very curious situation. Mr. White was a lawyer and interested in the whole problem of hypnotism in crime.

"Do you think hypnotism is dangerous?" he asked the subject.

"I'm sorry but I know nothing about hypnotism," came the puzzled reply.

"But you were hypnotized only five minutes ago."

"Now you're having your little joke, but I have never been hypnotized in all my life."

"I certainly saw you in hypnotism right in this room not five minutes back."

"You certainly saw no such thing. I know nothing about hypnotism, never have been hypnotized, and know that no one could put me to sleep."

It is a very curious thing that, with the use of the post-hypnotic suggestion, we can remove from the subject all knowledge of ever being in the trance. We merely assure him in hypnotism, "In future you will have no memory of ever being asleep. You will remember nothing about hypnotism but will insist that you have never been hypnotized in all your life"

After such a suggestion has been repeated a few times the subject has no knowledge of going into trance. We seat ourselves opposite him at the table. He is hypnotized and we talk along for half an hour. Then we awaken him and he at once picks up the conversation where he left off before being hypnotized. We ask him about the trance and he looks puzzled. He is quite sure that we have been talking quietly in our chairs ever since he entered the room. When he is told that he was in the trance, and is a good subject, he is inclined to think that we are trying to play a very poor joke on him. He reacts in exactly the same way as would the reader if his doctor were suddenly to enter the room and tell him that for the last hour he had been walking in his sleep. The whole thing doesn't make sense and the subject says so.

We can go even farther with the posthypnotic suggestion. Not only can we, with its aid, remove all knowledge from the subject of ever having been hypnotized; we can make it impossible for anyone beside the operator to hypnotize him at any future date. This again is the result of suggestion in the hypnotic trance. After such a suggestion the subject, no matter how good a somnambulist he may have been, becomes the most obstinate of all people when we try to get the trance.

In the waking state he not only denies that he has ever been hypnotized but is very unwilling for anyone to try and induce the trance. He claims that hypnotism is something he never liked, that he thinks the whole thing silly and does not wish to make a fool of himself. If we press him, he will consent very reluctantly to allow someone present to try, but the operator in question can get nowhere. The subject is definitely hostile and merely goes through the motions of co-operation but nothing more.

Finally, to complete this curious picture we use the posthypnotic suggestion to induce hypnotism, after the first trance. We say to the subject, "Listen carefully. In future, whenever I take the lobe of my left ear in my left hand and pull it three times, you will at once go sound asleep." This suggestion may have to be repeated several times, depending on the subject, but with a little practice it will work. To hypnotize the patient, the operator now merely strokes his left ear three times and the subject is in trance. Needless to say, we may use any cue, as long as we make it clear to the subject what this cue is to be. We may say to him, "You are asleep" or may use any other phrase as "Mary had a little lamb," if we wish it to be verbal, while the range of visual cues is unlimited.

The resulting picture of hypnotism is something with which the reader will be quite unfamiliar. We will see later that hypnotism has nothing to do with sleep, a good subject may be in deepest trance yet behave for all the world as if he were wide awake. For example, the writer has used a somnambulist as his bridge partner for an evening, had the subject play every other hand in the trance state and no one in the room was any the wiser. Control of the trance was exercised by means of post-hypnotic cues, in this case scratching the left ear or scratching the right ear to hypnotize or awaken the subject.

This shift from waking to hypnotic states can be extremely quick and subtle. The writer recently saw a very beautiful demonstration. Another operator was demonstrating with a very good subject, hypnotizing and awakening him, with the writer trying to detect the change. It turned out to be quite impossible, so well concealed were the cues and so quickly did the change occur. The only way the writer could decide was to ask the subject, quite frankly, "Are you asleep?" and take his word. In the last analysis it would have been easy to check up by using some test, such as anaesthesia, but under the circumstances this was not necessary. The subject was quite honest and enjoyed the game as much as anyone. This certainly is a very different picture of hypnotism from that which exists in the mind of the average layman. It is this very confusing, one might almost say, deceptive aspect of hypnotism to which we later devote several chapters.

We have noted the main points of interest in the posthypnotic suggestion. Anything which we can get in hypnotism we can get by posthypnotic means. We pointed out the weird compulsive power which these delayed suggestions have, especially when the subject does not realize the cause of his actions; also that the subject will tend to rationalize, to give reasons for his actions. These reasons he believes just as much as if they were genuine.

Then we have the curious fact that with the posthypnotic suggestion we can remove all knowledge of ever having been hypnotized and render it impossible for anyone but the operator to use hypnotism at any future date. Finally we can use posthypnotic cues to aid in hypnotizing at a future date. These can be employed so cleverly that an experienced operator cannot detect their use, cannot even detect, without tests, that the subject is in the trance.

There are a few other questions which seem of interest to the public. How long will the posthypnotic suggestion last? Frankly we have no idea. Liébeault reports a case in which a very complicated suggestion was carried out after a year. The writer recently ran across a case where the posthypnotic suggestion seemed to be fairly strong after twenty years.

During the last war he was interested in the study of hypnotism and was far more inclined to go in for "stunts" in those early days. He had a favorite trick with one subject. He would say, "Watch the front." Whereupon the subject would stand up and shout, "Call out the guard. Here comes Paul Revere."

It happened that recently the operator met this subject and in the course of the conversation suddenly said, "Watch the front." The subject looked puzzled, then said, "Call out the guard. Paul Revere is coming." Then he immediately looked even more puzzled and added, "I wonder why I said that. Somehow something you said recalls the last war and all the muck in the trenches. I never recalled the whole thing quite so vividly before."

We generally accept the fact that these suggestions tend to wear off unless we give some very specific time and date as four o'clock, Christmas afternoon, 1941. However with occasional reinforcement in the hypnotic trance there seems no reason why the posthypnotic suggestion would not last indefinitely. It seems to do so in the treatment of alcohol and tobacco. It is reasonable to suppose that it will do so in other situations.

The statement was made at the beginning of this chapter that any of the phenomena which could be obtained in hypnotism or by the posthypnotic suggestion could also be produced by means of autosuggestion. This is literally true but it is by no means as easy to demonstrate as are the various conditions we obtain in direct hypnosis. However, it can be shown quite conclusively if we use hypnotism as a "spring board" and reinforce or initiate the autosuggestion by suggestions given in the hypnotic trance.

Perhaps the general public is most familiar with autosuggestion through the works and lectures of the Frenchman, Coué. This man spent most of his life in Nancy, France, home of Liébeault and Bernheim, fathers of modern hypnotism. Actually he was neither a doctor nor a psychologist, but only the proprietor of the "corner drugstore," so to speak. However, living in that city with its traditions of achievement in hypnotic research, he picked up a considerable knowledge of technique, if not of theory.

Autosuggestion, as explained by Coué, was nothing new. Bernheim was quite familiar with all the phenomena he describes as we can see by reading his book *Suggestive Therapeutics*. However Coué had somewhat of the showman's technique and probably did psychology considerable service by bringing this phase of suggestion more to the attention of the public. His own writings are not convincing but, if the reader should be interested in following the subject further after our discussion in the following pages, we would refer him to the work by Baudouin *Suggestion and Autosuggestion*.

Let us first consider autosuggestion as initiated in the hypnotic trance. For example, we say to the subject, after he has seen an imaginary black dog in hypnotism, "Listen carefully. In the future whenever you wish to see the black dog when you are awake, you have only to take a pencil and a piece of paper, print the word 'dog' and the dog will appear before your eyes." We repeat these instructions carefully and then awaken the subject.

When awake, we say to him, "By the way, have you ever had a vision?" He admits he has not. "Well, how would you like to have one?" He says it would be a very interesting experience, so we hand him a pencil and paper, then say, "Now print the word 'dog' on the paper and tell me what you see." He does so and expresses great surprise at seeing a black dog standing beside his chair. This little trick may not succeed the first time, but given a good subject, and the repetition of the suggestion in several séances, we can usually count on success.

The various implications of this technique are fairly obvious. The writer recalls one very good subject who was troubled with inability to sleep. He was instructed in several séances that in future when he wished to sleep he would relax and repeat the first five letters of the alphabet "a" through "e." He would then have an irresistible impulse to go sound asleep and would remain asleep for as long as he wished.

This particular subject became so very good at this game that he was quite willing to show off his abilities before anyone. He would guarantee to go asleep on ten seconds' notice in spite of anything we could do, physical violence excepted. Not only that but it would be quite impossible to awaken him until he decided to awaken, say at the end of some fifteen minutes or half an hour.

The use of very specific autosuggestion to reinforce hypnotic and posthypnotic suggestions has, in our opinion, great possibilities. For example, we take a subject who complains of great difficulty in concentrating. He wishes to attend night school and does so, but finds it very hard to concentrate on his work after a day at the office. We try the usual hypnotic suggestions with considerable success, then clinch the matter with some very specific suggestions which are to take the form of autosuggestion.

We say to him, "In the evening when you wish to concentrate, you will prepare all your work so that you will not have to leave your room. You will then put your watch on the table, take a card and print on it 'Concentrate until 10:30.' You will place this card beside the watch. From then on you will have no difficulty whatsoever in attending to your work. Everything will leave your mind except the determination to work hard until 10:30 or whatever time you may print on the card." This little trick seems to help very much in securing the much desired ability to concentrate.

Here, of course, arises a very neat point. Is this actually autosuggestion or posthypnotic suggestion? In this book we will side-step the issue by saying that the question is only of theoretical interest. We could argue indefinitely over many such problems, as, for instance, is all suggestion autosuggestion or is all suggestion hetero-suggestion, that is, suggestion with the aid of an operator, real or imagined? The reader may feel he has the answer but we can assure him that much ink has been shed on this issue and it is still an open question. For our purposes we are entitled to avoid such problems on the plea that we simply go "round and round the mulberry bush." If the professional psychologist can not find the answer, we can not hope to do so.

As with the hallucination, we can obtain all other hypnotic phenomena by means of autosuggestion and by using the same technique. Paralyses, anaesthesias, even control of the heart rate lend themselves to this attack. But its real practical use would be in giving man command over himself, over his powers of concentration, and over his personality, so that he could rebuild himself along the lines of success and happiness. There may be here a great future for autosuggestion.

However, all autosuggestion need not be initiated by hypnotism. Coué was not interested in this approach and Baudouin outlines in his book very carefully the ordinary procedure. This is literally to give to yourself, when relaxed, the desired suggestions. Coué's famous formula, "Every day and in every way I'm getting better and better," was quite the rage a few years ago. Undoubtedly such a general formula can be of great help in many cases.

Coué in his writings on autosuggestion stresses the importance of imagination. If we can imagine a thing vividly enough, then it's true. This point is very open to argument. We must realize that in autosuggestion, as in hypnotism, people probably vary greatly in their openness to such suggestions. Success will not be uniform with any technique, some people will get results, others will not.

Nevertheless, the writer has found that the following procedure seems to be the one which is easiest and which can produce most of the things we get in hypnotism. The subject should relax on a couch or in a chair, close his eyes, and "Talk sleep" to himself. With a little practice he will recognize the coming of hypnosis, that "faraway" feeling accompanied by numbness in the limbs and a general laziness.

When this stage arrives the subject should then shift over to active suggestion, but without awakening himself. He must suggest to himself that, let us say, all sensation has gone out of his right arm or that he is listening to a symphony. The technique of autosuggestion is difficult, but it can be mastered. Once the subject has obtained this mastery he will find that not only can he produce, say, hallucinations in the trance itself but can actually suggest posthypnotic hallucinations to himself It does sound weird but it can be done.

For example, the writer while in military hospital had ample time to experiment with autosuggestion. He was able to suggest to himself that he would wake up at 2 A.M. and hear a symphony. Even more interesting he could suggest that he would awaken and hear spiritistic raps. Sure enough at 2 A.M. he was wide awake listening to very distinct raps from the spirit world.

Then came a very interesting experience, almost a state of divided consciousness. He heard the raps distinctly but knew they were the results of autosuggestion. He was even able to make a "mental request" that they group themselves in twos and threes and the spirits obliged. We will see later that hypnotism provides us with a key to explain most psychic phenomena, when these are genuine and not the result of magician's tricks.

Autosuggestion gives us an excellent device with which to study many strange things. The writer had a pet polar bear which he was able to call up merely by counting to five. This animal would parade around the hospital ward in most convincing fashion, over and under the beds, kiss the nurses and bite the doctors. It was very curious to note how obedient he was to "mental" commands, even jumping out of a three story window on demand.

But there is a certain menace to autosuggestion which this phantom bear illustrated. He became so very familiar that he refused to go away. He would turn up in the most unexpected places and without being sent for. The writer was playing bridge one evening and almost threw his hostess into hysterics by suddenly remarking, "There's that damn bear again. I wish someone would shoot the beast." He also had a nasty habit of turning up in dark corners at night, all very well when one realized he was just made of ghost-stuff but rather hard on one's nerves for all that. So he was banished and told never to return, but it was fully a month before the writer felt quite sure that his ghostly form would not be grinning at him over the foot of his bed during a thunderstorm.

There is a real danger here in connection with autosuggestion—a much greater menace than can ever arise from straight hypnotism. In the latter, the situation is always in skilled hands. Any bad effects can be remedied on the spot once and for all, but this is not so with autosuggestion. The subject is his own doctor, which has all the dangers this would imply if he were allowed the run of a drugstore to treat his ills without previous training. It is very hard for the average man himself to recognize trouble which may be the result of autosuggestion and just as difficult for him to treat it.

The writer recalls the case of a very gifted lady who became interested in spiritism. As we will see, the spiritistic phenomena are largely due to autosuggestion. She became so completely deranged through talking to the spirits—St. Augustine in this case—that she had to retire to a sanatarium. She has since regained a certain amount of her former mental balance but, left to herself, she could never have handled the situation. This was largely because she did not realize how very near she was to complete insanity. St. Augustine was a very real person, she valued his friendship immensely and resisted treatment until the supposed spirit was ousted by hypnotism. With this aid she recovered sanity enough to see how serious her situation was and from then on could help herself.

The writer cannot become very enthusiastic about autosuggestion. We will see in later pages that it may easily result in dissociation. In theory the subject should be able to guide his own treatment and become the master of his own personality. But it may just as readily encourage a tendency to dissociation which is latent in so many people, and with this lead to the development of neurotic traits which are far from desirable. The reader will do well to read through the next two chapters before he passes judgment on this statement. As yet we have not talked enough on the theory of hypnotism to give us a proper basis for discussion.

Anything which occurs in hypnotism or the posthypnotic suggestion we can get in autosuggestion. Finally any of these hypnotic phenomena may occur in everyday life, when we refer to the individual as "queer," an hysteric, a neurotic, even as insane. For this reason hypnotism is of very great importance, and we refer to it as the "laboratory" of abnormal psychology. It provides us with a key whereby we can under-stand the insane, and the neurotic.

For instance, the operator can suggest to a subject that, on awakening, he will have an irresistible impulse to kill every cat he sees, telling him in hypnotism that cats spread bubonic plague through their fleas and that by killing cats he will confer a great service on humanity. When the subject awakens he may very easily have an urge to kill any cat he meets. Asked for a reason he will insist that they are a menace to the country, that they spread the plague. Yet he will have no idea of where this idea comes from.

Should we run across such a case in everyday life we would say that he is suffering from a "compulsion." Actually we do have many examples of these compulsions as in the case of the kleptomaniac who must steal even worthless objects, the pyromaniac who must set fires, and many others. Moreover, we will point out in later pages that the kleptomaniac, and the pyromaniac are really working under a posthypnotic suggestion —minus the hypnotist. They act in exactly the same way as if they had been hypnotized and given their instructions in the trance. As a matter of fact we will see that they *have* been hypnotized at some time in their life and have been given the suggestion in question. The fact that no hypnotist was involved, that they may never have seen a hypnotist in all their life, we will see, has no bearing whatsoever on the case.

Similarly hypnotism gives us the explanation for many other types of mental disorder. The man who has a fear of cats, a phobia as it is called, acts exactly as if he had received the suggestion in hypnotism. And he did—only it was not labelled hypnotism. Likewise we will point out that an understanding of hypnotism helps us to understand "Napoleon" in your nearest state hospital for mental diseases. We can procure him in any psychological laboratory, and in so doing understand how he "gets that way" in normal life. As a matter of fact, the writer can see no difference between the Freudian complex and the posthypnotic suggestion. We will be in a better position to understand that statement after the next two chapters, but we would like to re-emphasize the thread of continuity. Hypnotism, posthypnotic suggestion, autosuggestion; what we get in one we can get in the other. And the phenomena we obtain in any of them occur in everyday life, when we refer to them as various mental disorders. But actually we can best understand them as forms of the posthypnotic suggestion or autosuggestion. This is why our subject is so very important.

Just a final word. Hypnotism may explain many forms of insanity. That does not mean to say that hypnotism can cure them. In some cases it may help, but the fact is that, while we may know why Mr. Smith is in hospital and thinks he is Napoleon, this does not guarantee a cure by hypnotism or any other means.

Chapter IV

SOME CURIOUS STATES IN EVERYDAY LIFE WHICH ARE DUE TO HYPNOTISM

L ET us now examine some of those states which are closely related to hypnotism, for in so doing we will not only understand the underlying cause of these related phenomena but will obtain a fuller picture of hypnotism itself. Take, for instance, automatic writing as a first example. The reader is probably familiar with this curious state, wherein the subject's hand writes "automatically" with no reference to what is in the conscious mind.

This may take many forms. The subject may lose consciousness completely while the hand writes, but in general he retains his full conscious faculties. He may be able to interrupt the hand but again the writing hand is generally a law unto itself. It scribbles along until it has finished, perhaps in five minutes, perhaps in fifty, then stops and is again a part of the normal body pattern.

The usual picture is somewhat as follows. The subject relaxes in a chair with a pencil in his hand, a paper on the desk. After one or two minutes the hand makes a few convulsive movements, then starts writing. The letters are generally large and ill-formed, but in some cases as in that of Stainton Moses the writing may be beautiful. The hand guides itself largely by touch and writes until it comes to the end of the page, then pauses with pencil uplifted awaiting a fresh sheet of paper. The subject himself may supply this with his other hand, or, if in trance, his associate will put the fresh sheets in place.

The strange thing about this whole procedure is that the subject has no control over the hand in question. He has not the slightest idea as to what it will next write and is often badly embarrassed when the hand makes a "remark," so to speak, which should not occur in polite society. We can screen the writing hand from the subject's sight, passing it through a cloth curtain. Then the subject can quietly read a magazine while we experiment with the hand. It will write along, in no way disturbing the subject and in no way disturbed by what he may be reading or thinking.

We stick a pin in the hand, but the subject does not pay the least attention. But the hand promptly writes "stop it," "cut it out," or some such phrase. The writer had an ex-army friend on whom he tried this little trick. Everything was going along in fine fashion until we pricked the hand with a needle, whereupon the hand burst into a stream of cuss words that would have made any regimental sergeant-major blush with shame. For full five minutes it told the operator just where he could go and how to get there. All this time the subject was reading *Oil for the Lamps of China* without the slightest idea that his good right arm was fighting a private war.

We refer to automatic writing as an example of dissociation. The arm in question is dissociated, is cut off from the rest of the body. This must mean that those parts of the brain which control the arm are for the time being disconnected with those parts responsible for normal waking consciousness, which could be explained in terms of the synapse theory we have already mentioned. At any rate, the arm acts by itself and seems to be an outlet by which the unconscious mind can express itself without completely unseating the conscious mind. Certain we are that this hand will often mention facts which are quite unknown to the subject.

This often has great use in medicine. We take a subject, aged twenty-five, who is a victim of the hand-washing mania; he simply must wash his hands forty times a day. He also does automatic writing, and as we can get no real information from him which might explain his compulsion to hand washing, we ask the hand itself in automatic writing.

"Why do you have this compulsion to wash?"

"I don't know."

"Now, think. When did it first make its appearance?"

"Sometime when I was about eleven or twelve."

"That is not close enough. You can do a lot better. Now, think. When? When and why?"

"Good heavens. Now I know," and the hand scribbles out the story. It appears that, as a boy, he had a dog of which he was very fond. On one occasion this dog fell into an open cesspool, and was in danger of drowning. The boy had a friend hold his legs, then reached down and rescued the dog, getting himself filthy in the process. Worse than this he also collected a sound thrashing from his father, who told him that he had probably contracted various diseases, including syphilis. On this basis was built up the morbid compulsion to wash his hands. We will see later that the most important step in curing many such conditions is that of learning the original cause.

We can find examples of these automatic movements in much simpler form than those involved in automatic writing. Most of the readers have probably been present at a "table tilting séance," wherein the table is in contact with the spirit world and raps out its messages to friends on this side of the border.

Science now generally concedes that the movements of the table are due to automatic—and quite unintentional—pushes and pulls on the part of the "sitter." The fact that these always protest that they have exerted no conscious effort means nothing, for we get these automatic movements in far more elaborate form with automatic writing and here the subject may be totally ignorant of what his hand is doing. Moreover, the plea that the table sometimes raps out information of which no one present is conscious also means nothing. These automatic movements, as coming from the unconscious, would have much material at their disposal of which the normal mind would be in ignorance. It is difficult for the average reader to grasp this possibility, but we will refer him to the cases of multiple personality which we discuss in later pages of this chapter. This weird condition probably gives the most convincing illustrations which psychology can muster.

In this same class, of course, comes work with the ouija board, an instrument with which we are all familiar. Here the automatic and wholly unconscious movements of the sitter guide the little table over the board as it spells out answers to the various questions. It is interesting to note here that some people can work the ouija board with great success obtaining from it all kinds of information of which they have no knowledge. It comes from the unconscious. Others can get nothing at all from the board. It simply refuses to budge. This is in strict accord with what we would expect if susceptibility to these automatic movements had anything to do with a similar openness to hypnotic suggestion.

And it has, very definitely. The writer, in his experience, has met many people who, as a pastime, practiced automatic writing. Whenever he has tried hypnotism with these people, they always turned out to be excellent subjects. And we find the same with people who can get good results from the ouija board. As a matter of fact an experienced operator has to waste very little time looking for subjects. A little inquiry will show that in any group there are people who consistently walk or talk in their sleep, who have practiced automatic writing, who like to work with the ouija board or who have success as "crystal gazers." With such people the operator can proceed under the almost certain assumption that he is dealing with good hypnotic subjects.

He is dealing with a person who is highly suggestible and it would appear that most of these automatic movements, so often associated with spiritism are largely the result of autosuggestion. The subject becomes interested in spiritism, and has an intense desire to get some of the "mediumistic" phenomena in himself. So he seats himself in front of paper, with a pencil in his hand, relaxes and hopes for results. This is simply one form of autosuggestion and if the individual is a good hypnotic subject, he gets the results he wishes. If not, he becomes discouraged and concludes that the whole thing is a fraud. But there is nothing supernatural or supernormal about automatic writing or the ouija board.

The results depend on dissociation produced by suggestion. We will see later that while dissociation may not be the whole explanation of hypnotism, the fact remains that we almost never get hypnotism without dissociation. They are psychological Siamese twins born of the same parent, suggestion, and both dependent on the suggestibility of the individual in question. That analogy is not quite correct, but it gives a pretty good picture for all that.

Then again we see the relationship between these states and hypnotism in the fact that we can easily obtain them in most good hypnotic subjects by means of suggestion in the trance. We make use of the posthypnotic suggestion, saying to the subject, "In the future whenever you wish to do automatic writing, you will sit down before a sheet of blank paper, take a pencil in your hand, and relax. You will then recite the first five letters of the alphabet at the end of which your hand will begin to write." It may be necessary to repeat these suggestions in following séances, even to give some very specific suggestion as "your hand will write 'Mary had a little lamb'" just by way of getting the subject into the knack of the thing. But with persistence the somnambulist can generally succeed with automatic writing while the automatic writer will almost always become a somnambulist.

Another curious phenomenon we see in everyday life is "crystal gazing." Here again the unconscious seems near the surface and in this case vision is used as the outlet. Also it can be obtained as a result of posthypnotic suggestion and very probably most crystal gazers are good hypnotic subjects. The writer has had too little experience here to say but feels certain that such is the case.

By the way, we do not need a crystal for crystal gazing. A glass of water is just as good especially if we have a point of concentration on the surface, such as a small drop of oil. Even this is unnecessary. And the technique for developing the "power" is exactly the same as is that in the case of automatic writing. Sit down, relax, gaze into the water, and hope for results, all of which is a perfect setting for autosuggestion. The process can be made much shorter by using the posthypnotic suggestion, showing again the close tie-up between the hypnotic states and these odd conditions of everyday life.

Moreover, the "visions" we get in crystal gazing are the same as the revelations through automatic writing. Material drawn from the unconscious mind, sometimes dealing with events of which the subject has no conscious knowledge. The reservoir is the same but the "pipe line" leads in different directions. In automatic writing to the hand, in crystal gazing to the eyes, but nothing supernatural in either case. A very excellent and authoritative book on this subject is that by T. Besterman.

All these conditions illustrate a very important principle of which we will later deal at greater length. Certain experiences of childhood and later life are "repressed," are forced out of consciousness because of the fact that they are very unpleasant. These are completely forgotten so far as our everyday life is concerned, but while "down" they are not "out." As a matter of fact, they may cause a great deal of trouble, being the origin of all sorts of mental disorders.

"Shell shock" is a case in point. It really should be called "war neurosis" since it has nothing to do with shells necessarily, but is a reaction to fear. In general, it will be found that these shell shock cases have a period of amnesia, a memory blank, for some very terrible experience. They remember nothing about it, yet for purposes of a cure it is necessary that it be restored to consciousness. Hypnotism is excellent, or any other trick, which taps the unconscious, including crystal gazing.

The writer recalls one such case in the last war. The patient was suffering from a violent tremor all over his body, so violent that he could not walk or even feed himself. The doctor, thinking that he would try hypnotism, began explaining to the subject just what he would want. In the course of the conversation the subject volunteered the information that he had once been very much interested in crystal gazing and had been quite successful in obtaining visions. This seemed a good lead so the doctor proposed he try it and report his experiences.

The patient did so, and saw in the glass the whole terrible experience of a bombing attack in which most of his company had been killed and he himself had bombed three of the enemy in a dugout under very harrowing circumstances. Yet previous to this vision he would not recall any details of the attack, his mind being a complete blank for a period of roughly twenty-four hours.

Another type of automatic activity which is not so generally known but which further illustrates our point is the phenomenon of "shell hearing." We are all familiar with the fact that if we cover an ear with a shell we get a peculiar confused roaring. In some people this roaring refines itself into voices and these become a series of auditory hallucinations. Moreover, we do not need the classic shell. A tea cup held over the ear does just as well and as usual the voices heard tell of events with which the subject is already familiar or which are in his unconscious mind.

Both automatic writing and shell hearing naturally lend themselves to another line of activity. The writer or listener is able to express his own philosophy of life in such a way that he may easily rank himself as a prophet. For some strange reason the average man is very much impressed with these automatic phenomena both in others and in himself. Consequently if he has a vision, receives a message by automatic writing or hears "voices" with or without the "shell," he is very liable to regard them as direct from the supernatural and act as if he were receiving guidance from the deity.

All the aspects of automatic phenomena are summed up best in our final example, automatic speech, speaking with tongues or glossolalia. The best book on the subject is that by G. B. Cutten. We are all familiar with the Bible story of Pentecost day, when the tongues of fire descended on the disciples' heads and they began talking in "tongues." Whether or not this original experience involved actual foreign languages in which they were to preach the reader may judge for himself. Suffice it for our purposes to say that fifty years later, in the days of St. Paul, the "gift of tongues" was understood by no one. St. Paul himself advises his followers to expend their energies along other lines since no person can understand what they are talking about. Since his time there has not been a case, acceptable to psychology, wherein an individual has been able to speak any language without first going through the process of learning the same. To be sure, we have heard of many such cases in popular literature, even have certain religious groups who insist that their members talk all sorts of foreign languages with no previous training, but the psychologist would still say "unproven."

What happens here is exactly the same sort of thing we have already seen in automatic writing. A case of dissociation, only here it is the muscles of the throat which are no longer under control of the normal waking personality. The individual starts talking just as the automatic writer writes, the throat muscles appearing to run themselves without any conscious control from the person in question. The words the subject utters may be utterly unintelligible, a language of his own, a "divine language" as it is sometimes called or he may speak his own native tongue, expressing what is in the unconscious mind.

In this latter case we again have an analogy from automatic writing. The thoughts expressed may be utterly trivial, even foolish, or they may represent the working of a profound, even artistic mind. It might be well here to introduce a case which achieved considerable fame a few years back, fame which was justly earned, to illustrate some points.

We refer to the case of Patience Worth. Here we have a lady, Mrs. Curran in everyday life, who lived the healthy normal existence of millions of other American women. She had a high school education, had early hoped to become a singer or an artist of some description and again, like millions of others, had been forced to realize that she simply did not have the ability. Fortunately she had the good sense to accept this fact, a point of view which all too many humans never will realize.

But, strange to say, Mrs. Curran ended up as an artist, one of the best; yet not Mrs. Curran, but the unconscious of Mrs. Curran, Patience Worth. This curious situation illustrates very nicely how these automatic phenomena merge into one another just as do the various stages of hypnotism. Table tilting and the ouija board are more or less crude manifestations of the unconscious at work, an outcropping which is not too convincing and is purely temporary, but in the case of Patience Worth the unconscious has assumed the role of a separate and distinct personality, one which is in some respects far superior in ability to the original. Here we are verging on multiple personality, which we will discuss very shortly.

This organized unconscious of Mrs. Curran gave itself the name of Patience Worth and claimed to be the spirit of an English girl who had lived in the reign of Queen Elizabeth, during the latter half of the sixteenth century. Moreover, while Mrs. Curran had no particular artistic ability, Patience Worth was an author of the highest grade, writing several books and publishing many poems which are admitted good by our best critics. And, strange as it may seem, these books contain a much higher percentage of sixteenth century English than almost any other novel or poem written in America! If the reader wishes a thorough and scientific discussion of this case we refer him to the book, *The Case of Patience Worth,* by W. F. Prince.

While science will not accept the claim that a spirit from past years occupies the body of Mrs. Curran, science will admit that the case is very complex, showing to a very high degree that ingenuity of the unconscious so evident in hypnotism. This unconscious, having assumed the title Patience Worth, has been remarkably consistent, as shown by the fact that she always uses a preponderance of old English words in all her writings. We leave the reader the task of reviewing the evidence and deciding for himself whether or not she has proved her point.

This particular case illustrates another very interesting phase of automatic activity. With practice it sometimes becomes far more efficient, the unconscious itself becoming better organized. Patience Worth began her communications with the planchette, a crude form of ouija board. But this was a very slow and clumsy method for such a brilliant personality so she "graduated" to automatic writing. Even this proved too tedious so she now does her work by automatic speech. Moreover, she has the most remarkable control over this speech. She, Mrs. Curran, sits down and relaxes. Immediately Patience Worth comes to the surface and begins work on her latest novel or book of poems, Mrs. Curran being conscious all the time and literally attending to her knitting. Should the phone ring Mrs. Curran immediately answers it, takes over control of her throat and talks as Mrs. Curran. A minute later Patience Worth is dictating her book!

This evidence of unconscious ability is by no means as rare as many of the readers may think. We find it in many spirit mediums, a group whom we discuss later in this chapter. And, as would naturally be expected, we find it in certain hypnotic subjects when we take the trouble to look, sometimes the evidence of artistic ability approaching genius. After all, that is not so unreasonable as it may sound. We have repeatedly said that the subject in hypnotism is not "asleep." He is very much awake, but a different personality. We know that a great deal of genius in humanity is held down by social pressure; the individual does not dare give vent to his artistic talents for fear of making a fool of himself. But we also know that hypnotism may lift these "inhibitions," as we term them, in some cases freeing the subject in the sense that he cares very little for the opinions of his social group. Under these circumstances genius, if it exists, might have the chance of pushing to the fore. For instance, Coleridge claimed to have written *Kubla Khan* during his sleep, which was very probably a state of unconscious activity.

As we mentioned before, these automatic phenomena tend to merge into one another. Patience Worth, as the unconscious of Mrs. Curran, is so well organized that we may regard her as a separate personality, which brings us to the most curious of all these automatic, these semi-hypnotic conditions, that of multiple personality.

And with this field of multiple personality we find a gradual increase in complexity. The most simple cases we refer to as the fugue or flight. William James, reported on such cases, among the earliest in the literature. A man named Ansel Bourne lived in Boston. Suddenly he vanished and after careful search was given up as lost. Six months later a man in Philadelphia, who had been running a grocery store suddenly "woke up," gave his name as Ansel Bourne and asked to know what he was doing so far away from home. Apparently he had run his grocery business fairly well for six months while in this "unconscious" condition, his "secondary" personality taking charge and giving the appearance of normalcy.

Such a case is very simple. From here we can go to the type of case represented by Rou. Here the reader will see the very close resemblance between this particular type and somnambulism as seen in sleep walking. We have already pointed out the very close relationship between somnambulism and hypnotism. Rou was a poor boy of Paris, France, who lived with his mother, a small storekeeper. But Rou was in the habit of frequenting saloons where he was fascinated by the tales of sailors.

He longed to become a sailor himself and escape from his uninteresting world. Then something very curious began to happen. He would suddenly lose consciousness and start for the seacoast, doing all sorts of odd jobs to keep himself alive and fit. His unconscious had taken over control and decided to become a sailor. Then at the end of a day, a week, or a month, he would suddenly come to himself or "wake up" without the slightest knowledge of where he was or how he got there. He would be sent back to Paris and would be quite normal for a period, then once again he would have a fugue, would walk in his sleep, and start out for the coast. This case we will see is more complex than that of Ansel Bourne in that the subject had recurrent attacks.

We could devote many pages to other cases by way of showing their growing complexity but will proceed at once to a very interesting and complex example, which was carefully studied by Professor Morton Prince of Harvard. We refer to the famous Beauchamp case of multiple personality.

Miss Beauchamp was a young lady, a nurse in training at a Boston Hospital, when Dr. Prince was called in to take over the case because of very peculiar actions on the part of the lady in question. After long and careful study he made a very interesting discovery. Her body contained no less than four distinct personalities. When he first met her she was under the control of the personality he later called B1, or the Angel. As such, she was a very sickly, nervous, highly religious, over-conscientious type, easily tired and always worrying over the sins of humanity and her own lost state.

Then he made a further discovery. Another personality made its appearance, BIII, Sally, or the Imp. Sally was a totally different proposition. She was a girl of eight or nine, absolutely irresponsible, with tireless energy and apparently no conscience whatsoever. Sally was always present but generally as an unconscious personality, "squeezed" by the Angel, as she said. She knew everything that was going on and thoroughly hated the other personality which insisted on taking the body to church, or keeping it quietly in its room while she, Sally, could think of far more interesting things to do. This was because Sally could not generally get control of the body but as the condition became worse, as the dissociation became more marked, Sally found it easier and easier to take over charge and then, ah then, she had a delicious revenge.

The Angel loathed even the appearance of sin. Sally was not by any means so conscientious. One of her delights was to take the body out on a wild "party" including beer and young men. Then to suddenly withdraw, leave the body to the Angel and watch her squirm as she got herself back to the hospital. This case occurred in the early 1900's, when the morals of the country would make such a situation even worse than today.

Then again, Sally was tireless, the Angel fatigued very easily. Sally could go for a five mile walk and end fresh as a daisy. Five hundred yards would leave the Angel exhausted, so Sally would get control of the body, take it on a particularly long walk and then withdraw, enjoying the tortures which the Angel suffered in getting herself back home again.

The Angel also prided herself on being very neat, both as to clothes and to room. This gave Sally a glorious opening. When particularly displeased with the Angel, she would take over control of the body and then wreck the room, turning the drawers inside out and piling everything in a heap in the middle of the floor. All these little tricks Sally used as a club on the Angel. In other words, "don't take the body to church; or else———. Do as I say, and I'll leave you in relative peace, be obstinate and I'll 'turn on the heat'." The reader will please note that this is not a case taken from a novel, as Dr. Jekyll and Mr. Hyde, but is an actual situation reported by one of our ablest psychiatrists. If the reader wishes further details than those we give, we refer him to Dr. Prince's own book, *The Dissociation of a Personality.*

Dr. Prince then discovered that a third personality was

appearing; namely, BIV or the Woman. It is curious to note
that neither the Angel nor the Woman were actually conscious
of Sally's thoughts and actions. Sally communicated with them
or rather delivered her ultimatums by letter and Prince explained what it was all about. Neither were the Woman nor
the Angel conscious of each other. But Sally, from her position,
was aware of both thoughts and actions of the other two. As
we said before, these cases of multiple personality can be very
complex.

The Woman had a different personality from either of the
others. She was headstrong, vain and spiteful; moreover, she
also insisted on taking the body to such places as good stores
and good concerts, which Sally loathed. So Sally started a
campaign against this new menace, but discovered that the
Woman and the Angel were quite different people to handle.
She tried her tricks but they did not work. She made a jumble
sale of the Woman's clothes, and piled them on the floor. The
Woman promptly took Sally's toys and threw them into the
fire. The conflict was short and sharp, ending in an armistice
with both sides in a position of armed neutrality. Unfortunately
they both occupied the same body, so there were definite limits
to which either could go. Sally would cheerfully have cut off
the Woman's nose but she would have been literally spiting her
own face. It happened to be her nose as well.

Then Dr. Prince made another discovery, and here we find
again the tie-up between hypnotism and these various states of
dissociation. If he hypnotized either B1, the Angel, or BIV, the
Woman, he got a new personality, BII, which had all the
memories of both. Moreover, this new individual was a much
more evenly balanced person than the other two, more of a real
woman. This led Prince to conclude that this was the real Miss
Beauchamp, that the Angel and the Woman were only halves,
so to speak, of BII.

Yet whenever he awakened BII, he always got BI or BIV.
However, with persistence and by insisting in hypnotism that

BII should awaken with the memories of both the Angel and the Woman he finally succeeded in awakening BII as the real Miss Beauchamp. And Sally? She could not be included in the personality synthesis. By means of hypnotism she was robbed of her power to control the body and "squeezed" back into her corner until she would no longer trouble the real Miss Beauchamp. That involves a very neat question in ethics. Sally was a real personality. To what extent was Prince guilty of psychological murder, so to speak?

We would wish to make a point before we proceed, since we wish later to show more clearly how and why hypnotism is of such use in these cases; in reality they are caused by a form of hypnotism in the first place! We will see that emotional shock produces exactly the same results as hypnotism, that hypnotism may in reality be a form of emotional shock. We are not clear on this point, but we do know that shock gives us all the phenomena of hypnotism and vice versa.

If we read over the Beauchamp case or most other such cases we will see that the condition has been caused by some severe emotional strain. What actually happened in the Beauchamp case appears to have been somewhat as follows. A very severe period of fear in childhood ending about the age of seven in a bad fright received from the father. This "split" the personality into the Sally, or BIII and the BII parts. Sally remained the childish creature she was at that time as a "co-conscious" personality, while BII continued her development. Then around the age of eighteen came another great shock, this time in connection with her love life, when BII split into BI, the Angel, and BIV, the Woman.

The reader will recall that BI or BIV hypnotized gave BII. The cure consisted of binding these personalities together again by means of hypnotism in the BII stage and then in being able to make this personality strong enough so that it would still remain BII on awakening and not return to BI or BIV. But BIII or Sally had had too long and independent an existence.

It proved impossible to unite her personality with that of BII, so the only way of solving this problem was to repress her completely. Somewhat of a Chinese puzzle but a very interesting study accepted as true in all psychological circles.

When Dr. Morton Prince was investigating the Beauchamp case, a namesake of his on the west coast, Dr. W. F. Prince, was unwittingly making a very important contribution to this subject of multiple personality and its very close relationship to hypnotism. The reader must be careful to keep these two men separate for they were both friendly enemies during their entire lives. W. F. Prince passed his later years in Boston so that, with Morton Prince at Harvard, they could really quarrel to their hearts' content. Both, we should add, were men of the very highest ability, names that are respected and honored in the history of psychology.

Dr. W. F. Prince was probably America's greatest authority on psychic research or spiritism for the last ten or fifteen years before his death. Yet he conducted his research in this very difficult subject in such a way as to hold the respect of science. This is the more remarkable when we bear in mind the fact that his, of all fields, is open to suspicion of fraud, prejudice, and poor scientific methods. His writings, found among the publications of the Boston Society for Psychic Research as well as the American and British Societies, are always characterized by moderation and a keen sense of scientific judgment.

The unwitting contribution of W. F. Prince to this subject of multiple personality came about somewhat as follows. Dr. Morton Prince was receiving great publicity in scientific circles for his excellent work with Miss Beauchamp, and in the early 1900's very little was known about such cases. W. F. Prince in his ceaseless search for the one best spiritistic medium was working with a girl, Doris Fischer. He was astonished to find that Miss Fischer was also a case of multiple personality and, following the technique of the Harvard man, he used hypnotism to investigate his very interesting subject. To his astonishment and that of the world in general this case developed in almost identical fashion to that of Miss Beauchamp. There was a Sally, an Angel, and a Woman, although W. F. Prince did not use these names. Moreover in the course of the treatment he cured the condition in a fashion very similar to that used by Morton Prince. His Angel and his Woman were brought together as the real Miss Fischer through hypnotism, while his Sally was "squeezed" into oblivion. It is of interest to note that he adopted Miss Fischer as his own daughter and after the cure she gave every appearance of being a very healthy, well balanced personality.

The great significance of this case lies in the fact that W. F. Prince, one of the most careful investigators almost certainly created this case of multiple personality through the use of hypnotism, and this result was quite unintentional on his part. A striking example of the effects which operator attitude may have. We can visualize the process. Miss Fischer was an excellent hypnotic subject and of more than average intelligence. Morton Prince was just publishing his remarkable Beauchamp case. Dr. W. F. Prince, later her adopted father, was very much interested in this, doubtlessly the literature was lying around and he probably discussed the case in her presence. He certainly had in his own mind a very clear cut image of how the Beauchamp case was progressing.

When he began his work with Miss Fischer, somehow this picture was conveyed to the subject's mind, whether through her own reading, his discussion or through unconscious hints which he let drop. This is almost certain because these cases of multiple personality simply do not follow a fixed pattern. The many examples we have in the literature are extremely varied as to number and type of personalities. That these two most complex of all cases should be identical is almost impossible. The evidence is all in favor of the fact that the Doris Fischer case was built up on the spot.

In fact there are some who will go even farther and claim

that the Beauchamp case itself was at least guided in its development by the use of hypnotism. Even as late as 1905 or 1910 we did not know nearly as much of the importance which operator attitude may assume. If two men of this capacity could be completely deceived, the reader will see our reasons for questioning a great deal of the experiments reported by older investigators.

The work of the two Princes carries us still farther into this matter of hypnotism and multiple personality. It sheds some very interesting light on the problems presented by spiritism, their argument here centering around the famous spirit medium, Mrs. Chenoweth. The reader will find her work discussed at length by W. F. Prince and others in the proceedings of both the American and the British Societies for Psychic Research. She was probably the best "mental" medium in America outside the famous Mrs. Piper, at the time of this investigation an old lady.

Mrs. Chenoweth gave the typical picture of the spirit medium when in trance. She was controlled by the spirit of an Indian girl "Sunbeam" who had been killed by a fall from a horse in the West many years ago. Mrs. Chenoweth would sit at her table with the "sitter" on the opposite side. Then she would pass into the trance state and Sunbeam would come to take charge. She would chatter along at a great rate in a girlish voice until the sitter interrupted by reminding her that he was there for a purpose. Then she would suddenly come "down to earth" as it were and give the sitter information which was supposed to come from the spirit world.

Some of this was very hard to explain unless we admitted supernormal power on the part of the medium. For example, one of the writer's friends reports the following. Sunbeam said that she saw standing beside him the form of his father, now dead. The sitter naturally asked how he was to be sure it was his father. To this Sunbeam replied.

"He says for you to carry out the following directions as proof. Go home, go to the cellar, look up his diary for April 16,

1896. There you will find that he bought five acres of land from a Mr. Jones on Long Island." The sitter went home, looked up the date in the diary and found the entry as described. He says he had never looked into his father's diary.

Which proves that he was talking to his father? By no means. There are several other possibilities which might have explained it. The medium may have been a fraud, have gotten hold of the diary beforehand and so had the information, although this seems very improbable. Or the sitter may have an hallucination himself and have looked up the diary after the manner of post-hypnotic suggestion, rationalizing later as any good hypnotic subject will.

Fantastic? Possibly, but let us see what Dr. Morton Prince says. He was one of the world's best and he also lived near Boston, so that he could easily check up. And he did! His conclusions after investigating Mrs. Chenoweth were that she was a most interesting case of multiple personality—nothing more. "Sunbeam" was a sort of Sally and the other controls—for there were others—were merely the same thing he had already seen in the case of Miss Beauchamp. Certainly they were not visitors from the spirit world communicating with man through the body of Mrs. Chenoweth.

His opinion was thus in flat contradiction to that of W. F. Prince. To be sure, the latter was always very careful in his statements but the writer, who knew both these men, is convinced that Dr. W. F. Prince felt Mrs. Chenoweth did have supernormal abilities. Just how one would explain these abilities was a different matter, whether by spirit-intervention, telepathy, or clairvoyance, but he was convinced they existed.

Our point is this. Here we have possibly the two best men in the world as to qualifications investigating the best medium in America. Their conclusions were directly contrary, the one leaning towards an explanation only in terms of multiple personality, the other strongly inclined to see the supernormal in the revelations of the medium. If two men of this ability could not come to a solution of the problem, we must not expect too much from ourselves.

But we feel certain that we voice the vast majority of psychological opinion when we say that the mediumistic trance is nothing more than a state produced by autosuggestion, and as such is almost identical with the trance we see in somnambulism. Moreover, the various spirit controls are only manifestations of multiple personality, which again is so closely associated with hypnotism. We know that, with hypnosis, we can produce multiple personality. Hypnotism is also recognized as the best means to effect a cure. Furthermore, every case of multiple personality which has been subject to a psychologist's experimentation has always turned out to be an excellent hypnotic subject. If he does not prove to be such, we may take it for granted that he is bluffing—for an attack of multiple personality, a fugue such as that suffered in the case of Ansel Bourne, can be easily faked and affords the "patient" a beautiful "out" when home conditions become unbearable.

The writer was present when Professor William Brown of Oxford attempted to hypnotize one such case which had received wide publicity in the English press. Although one of the world's best operators, he had absolutely no success and promptly stated that he thought the subject had bluffed the whole thing. And such was probably the case.

It is quite impossible to discuss spiritistic phenomena at any length in a book devoted to hypnotism. Space does not permit. The writer had the opportunity of doing two years' fairly intensive work on psychic research while on scholarship at Harvard under the direction of the late Professor William McDougall and Professor Gardiner Murphy, now of City College of New York. If the reader chooses, he may look up reference to part of this work in the two excellent books of J. B. Rhine of Duke University, *New Frontiers of the Mind* and *Extrasensory Perception*. So the writer has at least a bowing acquaintance with the field and feels that his following statements would be regarded as fair by the vast majority of psychological opinion in the country.

First as to the existence of "spiritistic" phenomena. Definitely unproven. The writer would, however, place himself on record as being far more optimistic here than most of his colleagues. He insists that there are many reports of experiments and of occurrences which cannot be explained by the normal laws of psychology as we now know them. Further that it may be quite impossible to prove "spiritism" by the laboratory method. The cold scientific atmosphere which exudes from any professional psychologist may kill something essential to the manifestation of the supernatural. But that is only a personal opinion in which the writer realizes he is in a definite minority.

So first, "unproven." Secondly, why? Various reasons. Above all things, fraud. This is a commercial world and many people find it very easy to make a comfortable income by capitalizing on the desire which we all possess for absolute assurance of a life hereafter, for the ability to communicate with those we love who are now dead. The writer recalls one very interesting and amusing case. He was attending a spiritistic séance in London, England. During the course of this séance, which was held in very bad light, a chair travelled from one side of the room to the other with no visible means of propulsion. After the meeting came to an end he wandered over to the chair and noticed it had stopped over a hot air register. The answer was obvious. A string down the hot air vent was the cause of the movement.

At the next séance he arrived early and seated himself near the opening in question, hoping that the chair would repeat its performance. It did. So the writer kept his eyes glued on the chair convinced that sooner or later someone would untie a string. And they—or rather she—did. For when everyone's attention was concentrated on a guitar which was floating over the medium's table, a small hand clothed in a black glove stole out from behind a near-by curtain to untie the string. The

writer reached down and shook hands with no intention whatsoever of creating a scene. There was a ten second pause and
the owner of the hand suddenly thrust a needle into the unwel-
come hand. This hurt like sin so the writer squeezed and pulled,
dragging a lady into the middle of the floor. The light immediately went on, the medium had hysterics, and the writer left
at once by the window. Only on his way home did he realize he
had left his hat behind where it still resides to this day for all
he knows.

We divide the mediums into two broad groups: the physical
mediums and the mental mediums. With the physical medium
"things happen." Lights float around the room, music is heard,
forms materialize, and objects, such as chairs, tables, or guitars,
also float in mid air. Unfortunately these séances almost invariably take place in light so bad that it is impossible to detect
fraud if such exists. The medium claims that the spirit forces
cannot work in light. This is very unfortunate, for it also
makes fraud very easy. We would also point out that the
greatest of all physical mediums, D. D. Home, did his work
in broad daylight. He produced better phenomena than any
medium since, on one occasion floating out one window and
in another six stories up! And this in excellent light! Unfortunately he did his work over fifty years ago. No one has been
able to duplicate it since and so science is naturally sceptical.

We are probably on safe ground when we say that the work
of the physical medium does not deserve serious consideration
from science. No matter how good the "controls" in darkness
there will always be the suspicion of fraud. One English investigator recently tried to use the infra-red camera, which
takes pictures in darkness by means of rays invisible to the
human eye. But again the "spirits" became sensitive and de-
manded that it be withdrawn. Science cannot waste its time in
tiresome investigations under conditions which will always be
open to question.

The "mental" medium, on the other hand, gives us a somewhat different problem. Here it is a question of messages from the dead, of clairvoyance, or of telepathy. To be sure there is plenty of fraud among mental mediums but at least they meet us on a fair basis. They do not demand conditions which a priori make investigation impossible. We may divide this "mental" group into the fraudulent and the genuine. For an exposé of the method employed by the fraudulent medium we would refer the reader to two books, Abbott, *Behind the Scenes with the Mediums* and that by Price and Dingwall, *Revelations of a Spirit Medium.*

The genuine spirit medium is in a class by himself. There can be no doubt of his—or her—sincerity. The "trance" is genuine and the various spirit controls certainly act as if they had nothing to conceal. How, then, does psychology explain the results obtained by such great mediums as Mrs. Piper, Mrs. Leonard, or Mrs. Chenoweth?

In the first place the trance is an excellent example of auto-hypnosis. The spiritistic trance and the hypnotic trance are identical to all intents and purposes. One is induced by the subject himself, the other with the aid of an operator. Who are the spirit "controls" such as "Sunbeam" who take over the control of the body during these séances, reporting messages from the spirit world and describing the various dead friends whom we contact? Simply the various personalities in a case of multiple personality, which as we have seen is so closely tied up with hypnotism.

The messages we receive? That is another question. In the writer's opinion, a question with not nearly as convincing an answer as the first two. First, we have the matter of unconscious cues and the possibility of great sense acuity on the part of the medium, or at least great concentration on tiny details as we mentioned in the case where the subject finds his mother's "picture." Remember that the hypnotic and mediumistic trance are essentially the same. What applies to one will hold for the other. For example, the writer was conducting some card reading experiments with a very intelligent sitter. The subject, not in hypnotism, was trying to guess the playing card on which the operator was concentrating. The operator cut the jack of hearts and the subject immediately named the card correctly. Then he added, "I'm sure of that one."

"Why?"

"I heard you whisper it."

Yet the writer would have sworn he had made no sound. He found this occurring several times with this subject and also in isolated cases with other subjects. Now, in theory, this subject may have had very acute hearing quite apart from hypnotic or mediumistic trance. We know from psychology that thought generally involves tiny speech movements. The thinker literally "talks to himself." It might be that some people have such extraordinarily keen hearing that they could pick up these unconscious and very tiny sounds, so receiving some very valuable information. Farfetched, perhaps, but possible.

This also would apply to the sense of vision, even more so to the sense of touch. Some mediums ask to hold the sitter's hand. We all have at least heard of the marvelous ability of some people at "muscle reading." Suffice it here to say that this ability seems quite genuine and is accepted by psychology. Here the medium could possibly pick up expression of assent or dissent through muscle "twitches." This also may seem like a pretty difficult theory to accept, but it has its points.

More important, possibly, than either of these is the subject's recognition of changes in the sitter's face. Those subtle expressions which would tell her when she is "hot" or "cold," as she starts out to make a statement. Here again some people may have this power of discrimination developed to a very high degree, much higher than that found in the average.

Then again we find that some mediums are expert at "fishing" for information. They will throw out a hint or suggestion, watch the sitter's reactions very closely and immediately follow up with "No, that's wrong," if the sitter seems to register disapproval. If the suggestion is acceptable, they will at once follow up cautiously, feeling their way, fishing for information, and get results which are quite astonishing. All this without the sitter's being in any way aware of what is taking place.

The psychologist also has another very potent criticism against the sitter himself. The human memory is very unreliable. For a fine treatise on just how unreliable, read the book by Hugo Münsterberg, *On the Witness Stand*. We cannot accept any reports of a mediumistic séance unless a secretary was present and took down all the proceedings in shorthand.

The writer had a case which illustrated this in very fine style. A friend of his had a sitting with Mrs. Chenoweth. He came away enthusiastic reporting that the medium had given him fine evidence that she was actually talking with his father. The writer had this friend hand in a report on the sitting, and then proceeded to "work" on him for the next two weeks with a view to making him change his story. Certain parts were greatly magnified during various conversations, others were completely omitted, certain new details were seized on and inserted.

At the end of this two weeks period the sitter was asked for another report on the plea that the former one had unfortunately been lost. The two reports turned out to be very different, so different in fact, that they were quite worthless as evidence. The average sitter does not realize how unreliable his own memory is or how his memory of the séance may be changed by later additions and subtractions. So, in scientific investigation we always insist on a secretarial report of what has taken place at a sitting with the "mental" medium.

Yet, for all these objections, the writer still feels that there are many points which have not been cleared up. Read, for example, Podmore's *Phantasms of the Living*, or look up the sittings of Piper, Chenoweth, or Leonard in the proceedings of the various societies previously mentioned. The writer does not claim that they prove spiritism, even the supernatural but they certainly have not been explained away to his satisfaction. Also many experiments on straight telepathy included in these proceedings as well as evidence for clairvoyance. Whatever the explanation, they are not as yet explained. Nor are the results obtained by Rhine at Duke University to be brushed aside lightly as many of our critics seem to think. The waving of the magical psychological wand with the word "bunk" may satisfy the magician but not the audience.

In later chapters we will develop at greater length on this thesis of states closely related to hypnotism. For example, read Healy's book, *Mental Conflicts and Misconduct*. Bear in mind that emotion gives identical results with hypnotism and see how easily his cases of kleptomania or compulsive stealing fit into the picture of the posthypnotic suggestion. No hypnotist in his laboratory could have done better than nature "in the raw."

Indeed, so closely related is all functional insanity to the phenomena of hypnotism and suggestibility that the picture seems almost too simple. The compulsions, fears, and delusions of the insane and the neurotics look very much like the post-hypnotic suggestion while the so-called Freudian "complex" is literally its twin brother.

Crime, insanity, but most important of all, our everyday life. We can more or less isolate the two first in our jails and our asylums. At any rate we don't approve of criminals and the insane, but we do most sincerely approve of ourselves and our neighbors. And here, unfortunately, is where hypnotism does its most terrible damage. Consider the present World War. All the insanity and crime we have in this world of ours becomes a colorless grey compared to the lurid red of bursting bombs and torpedoes.

It has always been the writer's contention that Hitler is the greatest hypnotist of our day, and this statement is not just a play upon words. To be sure he may never have read a book on the subject or know the meaning of the word. We recall the gentleman in the old French play who was delighted to find he had been speaking prose all his life. We can I think, make out a very convincing case that basically Hitler's emotional domination of the crowd—or, speaking professionally, his attack, is only the attack of the stage hypnotist, one step removed. If we can only understand the laws beneath mob psychology, perhaps we can be happier and more useful in this sadly torn world of today. And then, again, perhaps we cannot. That will depend on ourselves.

Chapter V

THE BASIC NATURE OF HYPNOTISM

MAN is incurably a mystic. Ever since the day, some one hundred thousand years ago, that old Neanderthal man first began burying his dead, probably long before, man rolled his eyes in horror at the forces of magic and the spirits of the departed. After all, he had good evidence. He dreamed and in his dreams he saw his dead enemies, so they were still alive. His hazy thinking could not keep dreams and reality separated. Then again in his dreams he visited places many miles away, so obviously his spirit could leave his own body in sleep and travel long distances. These events were very real to him.

We have a story from Australia that on one occasion a tribe of friendly blacks suddenly swept down on a settlement, killing and burning in the most ferocious manner. Why? The medicine man had a dream. He was at the white settlement and the whites were preparing to attack them, their friends. He was so furious over this treachery that he promptly gathered all his followers together and tried to wipe out the whole lot. From his viewpoint he was quite right. His spirit had visited the white village and, after all, he could certainly believe his own eyes.

This may seem very silly to us but it was terribly real to our ancestors. With the Australian no death was natural, everyone died by magic. So when your brother died the medicine man, with his own magic, found out who killed him. Then it was your duty, as his brother, to carry on the "blood feud," and kill the culprit. His relations did the same and everyone was happy, for these old savages dearly loved the warpath.

One of the very worst tricks you could possibly play on your enemy was to move him or disguise him when he was asleep. In sleep the spirit left the body and wandered over the country. That was quite clear from dreams. So you waited until your opponent was sound asleep then quietly moved him to another house. Or just as good, you put a mask over his face. Then the returning spirit could not find the body to which it belonged and your hated enemy went insane, robbed of his soul. Ridiculous? Yes, but many a savage has died in quick violent fashion, for playing just such pranks on his neighbors.

Even Plato, the great Greek philosopher, agreed that anyone found sticking pins in a wax doll should be put to death. It was perfectly reasonable. No one would deny the power of magic. One of the best ways of killing your enemy was to make an image of him in wax then stick it full of pins. Better still, put the wax figure in front of the fire. As it gradually melted away he would weaken and die. Indeed only one hundred fifty years ago in Europe we find the hospital conditions terrible. The insane were chained in the filthy cells of Bedlam or other hospitals, sport for the public who were allowed to prod them with poles or stick them with pins. Insanity was the result of evil spirits and man could do nothing against these. God was punishing them for their sins, so man helped on the good work, making their lives a living tragedy.

We must always bear these facts in mind when we consider the history and the theories of hypnotism. Of all branches of science it was the most weird, lent itself best to a mystic explanation, as is evident even today. Many parents who would not hesitate to have their children's tonsils out tomorrow, if necessary, would be pretty horrified if the doctor suggested using hypnotism to cure, shall we say, nail biting. We are not so very far ahead of our head hunting ancestors.

And hypnotism, without doubt originated right back among such ancestors. Not as hypnotism, to be sure, but as part of their religious and mystic ceremonies. For example, in the initiation ceremony of the Chippewa Indians we have as fine a form of group hypnotism as the best operator could demand. The boys at initiation were lulled into this magic sleep by the chanting of the medicine man and there instructed in tribal customs. Some even developed anaesthesia to pain and later performed prodigies of valor without feeling their own wounds.

But this could hardly be classed as hypnotism, although it was indeed that. The Indian knew nothing of the scientific laws governing the state and while he used it most effectively it was always linked with the supernatural. So also were the sleep-temples of ancient Egypt. To these the sufferer would come, would be thrown into trance by the priest and while in trance would be visited by the various gods who were the patron saints of medicine. These temples later made their way into Greece and Asia Minor, and represent a very interesting stage in the development of hypnotism but contributed nothing. The practices used herein appear to have vanished completely with the arrival of the Christian era.

Then hypnotism and all its many related phenomena passed into oblivion, so far as actual practice was concerned. The Church had a hearty distrust of all such "black cults," linked them to the devil himself, and anyone practicing the same might easily find himself burning at a stake. We have some most interesting tales of persecution during the so-called dark ages, by the Catholic Church at first, but in later times by the Protestant Church and by the lay authorities themselves. We cannot fix blame for this on any one group. All humanity had an unreasoning fear of black magic and rooted it out with savage brutality.

One German story shows how, at least in one instance, the victim turned the tables on his persecutors in tragic style. A German was to be tried for sorcery. He was an alchemist, one of those very early chemists who were regarded as the blackest of the black. He realized he had no chance of escape, so wrote his daughter asking her to come and watch the fun.

Half a dozen judges presided at the trial under the chairmanship of a prince. The culprit was brought in and formally accused of being a wizard. He at once pleaded guilty, and that, so to speak, was that. But with the victim safely convicted his judges decided on getting some information. Very famous in these days was the "witch's supper" at which all these people were supposed to gather and plot against honest men. So one of the judges asked the victim, since he admitted his guilt, to tell them when the witches had last met.

"Sunday at midnight."

"Will you describe it to us?"

"I would gladly, but why waste time? You were there."

"I was not."

"You certainly were. You and these other two judges," singling out two more whom he particularly disliked. "Prince, I accuse these three men of wizardry." Then he went on to describe a weird scene in which he, the three accused, and the other witches were plotting to spread a terrible pestilence over the whole state. Result?

"Burn the lot of them," said the Prince.

We imagine that questions were a little more discreet from then on.

The scientific study of hypnotism begins with a Viennese doctor named Mesmer who lived during the American Revolution. As a matter of fact, Benjamin Franklin, as our ambassador to France, sat on a board of the French Academy of Medicine which pronounced Mesmer a fraud and drove him from Paris.

Actually this man was not a fraud in any sense of the word. His ideas are weird as we read them one hundred seventy years after his time, but Mesmer was probably quite sincere in all his statements. We must bear in mind that he lived at the dawn of medical science, at a time when Franklin himself said, "There are good doctors and bad doctors but the best doctor is no doctor."

In reality Mesmer contributed practically nothing to the science of hypnotism. Hull says, "His theories are of very considerable interest to the historian of the growth of science, perhaps not so much for the amount of truth they contained as because it has taken the world such a long time to separate the grain of truth from its enormous husk of error." [1]

The University of Vienna at that time had perhaps the world's best medical school. Here he wrote his medical thesis in 1766 on the influence of the planets upon the bodies of men! Today no medical school in the world would consider such trash, but times have changed. Then anaesthesia was unknown, the germ theory was still one hundred years in the future and insanity was the work of the devil. So we must judge Mesmer in the light of his times, a capable doctor who dared to blaze a new trail and who was master of the medical knowledge of his time, such as it was. To be sure he had a very shrewd financial eye and used his knowledge to fill his own purse. But that is not unheard of, even in this enlightened twentieth century.

Mesmer was a very keen observer. The principle of the magnet with its two poles was just being investigated. He noted that the magnet—like the planets—could exert its influence at a distance. So he worked out his theory. The human body, with its two sides, was like a magnet, with its two poles. Disease was caused by an improper distribution of the magnetic fluid, the animal magnetism which this living magnet threw off and to cure disease we had to restore the balance, so to speak.

This animal magnetism was a gas or fluid, therefore somewhat different from that of the minerals. It was under the control of the human will, hence to this day we have the tradition of "will power" in hypnotism. To direct its flow the individual must concentrate with all his strength and look his victim firmly in the eye. Hence the "dark hypnotic eye." Then as it flowed largely from the hand, the operator would make long passes over the body of his patient, from his head to his toes, passing the fluid into the sufferer's body. Should the sub-

---

[1] Hull, Clark L., *Hypnosis and Suggestibility*, p. 5.

ject go into a trance, he was awakened by reversing the process. The passes went from toes to head, so withdrawing the influence. Mesmer actually never got quite this far, but such was the standard practice of his immediate followers, the "Mesmerists," and we see many of these practices still used by the stage hypnotist.

In reality he had quite a lot to go on here, for the magnetic fluid was quite visible—to some people. Many "sensitives" could actually see it streaming from the eyes and hands of the operator. Of course, this was simply a visual hallucination, now so well known in hypnotism. But in Mesmer's time no one realized that such a thing existed so there was no reason to reject the word of those somnambulists who reported and described the fluid in question.

This fluid had many interesting qualities. It could be reflected by mirrors. It could operate at a distance. More interesting, it could be confined in a bottle and shipped to a sufferer in any part of the world. Most interesting of all any good "magnetist" could magnetize any object, generally a tree in the village green. Then the whole village could gather round this tree, receive the benefits of Mesmer's great discovery—and the operator collect his fee.

Mesmer's own clinic in Paris deserves special mention, for it must have been a remarkable sight. The large hall was darkened and soft plaintive music accompanied the treatment. Here was the famous *baquet,* a huge open tub about a foot high, large enough for thirty people to stand around for treatments. The tub itself was filled with water, bottles arranged in a symmetrical order, iron filings and ground glass. The whole thing was provided with a wooden cover and through this cover came jointed iron rods which the patients applied to their ailing parts. Mesmer himself would appear at the right moment in a robe of brilliant silk, passing his hands over the patients, fixing them with his gaze and touching them with his iron wand. People suffering from all kinds of sicknesses were cured after a few such treatments. This is, of course, exactly what we would expect from our present day knowledge of hypnotism.

Mesmer's success was probably his undoing, for he drew much trade away from the regular doctors. These only needed some excuse to vent their spleen and the opportunity came in 1784 for the French Government appointed a commission—including Franklin—to investigate the whole thing. This pronounced Mesmer a fraud. Immediately his popularity fell off and he left Paris shortly afterward. This verdict meant very little when we consider the ignorance of the eighteenth century doctor. Vesalius was almost burned at the stake when, a little before this time, he insisted on cutting up human corpses to study anatomy. After Leeuvenhoek discovered the microscope and described germs it needed two hundred years and the genius of a Pasteur for "science" to recognize that they might be of importance. So, even had Mesmer been right the verdict would probably have been the same. It so happened he was wrong—but honestly wrong.

But, as we said before, Mesmer contributed practically nothing to modern hypnotism. His theories were completely wrong and most of his pupils followed blindly in his lead. He did, however, "throw the fat in the fire," so to speak. Once he had invented his technique, it was almost impossible not to stumble on the phenomena of modern hypnotism. The fact that it took one hundred years for the story to unravel itself, and that we still know so little about many important phases merely illustrates the slow pace at which science must progress.

Mesmer did not hypnotize or try to hypnotize his subjects. Nevertheless some of then went into spontaneous hysterical convulsion as they received treatment around the tub. These convulsive attacks came more and more into the limelight. A report from the Royal Society of Medicine at this time says, "From a curative point of view animal magnetism is nothing but the art of making sensitive people fall into convulsions."

In 1784 one of Mesmer's pupils, the Marquis de Puységur,

stumbled across genuine hypnotic somnambulism. He "mag-
netized" a young shepherd, Victor, but this boy fell into a quiet
sleeping trance instead of into the usual convulsive attack. In
this state he went about his business and when he "awakened"
knew nothing of what had happened. This was something entirely new and, as such, immediately attracted great attention.
Mesmerism, by sheer accident was on its way to becoming hypnotism. To be sure the main interest in this new phenomenon
of somnambulism was mystic. The subject was supposed to
develop clairvoyant powers, to have the gift of thought transference, even to speak with the dead. At the same time the
mesmerists were getting dangerously near the truth, so near
that discovery of the real facts was just a matter of time. By
1825 hallucinations, anaesthesia and the posthypnotic suggestion had all been described.

Yet progress was painfully slow. One of the greatest figures
in these days was an Englishman named Braid. He did his
early work in the 1840's, first used the term hypnotism, rejected completely the idea of the magnetic fluid and saw that hypnotism
was something quite different from ordinary sleep. He also
invented an hypnotic technique, still used by many operators,
that of gazing at a bright object held in such a position as to
strain the eyes.

But we still find that weird mixture of truth and absurd
error. Phrenology was then in vogue and Braid supported the
theory known as phreno-magnetism. He found with his subjects that if he pressed the "bump" of pugnacity, the subject
would promptly want to fight, if it were that of reverence, the
subject might fall on his knees and pray. In his later writings
he saw the absurdity of these claims and even appears to have
hit the real keynote of hypnotism, namely, suggestibility. Braid
was more or less the voice of one crying in the wilderness. With
his death there was no further immediate interest in England.

The French, however, were more alert to possibilities. Around
1815, the Abbe Faria made a very important discovery. If the

prospective subjects were seated around the room and allowed to relax, then the operator had merely to repeat the word "sleep" several times in an impressive voice. Certain of those present would at once fall into somnambulism. This was a very important step and the French investigation finally ended in the work of Liébeault, the real father of modern hypnotism.

This man was one of those peculiar people who mark off the milestones in science. A physician, he settled at Nancy, France, in 1864. Here he proceeded to practice hypnotism among the poor, refusing any fees for his services. He even wrote a book, setting forth his theories on the subject—and sold exactly one copy.

But that did not discourage Liébeault. For twenty years he kept at his task. Then, fortunately, he won the enmity of a great French physician, Bernheim, a professor in the medical school at Nancy. Bernheim for six months had been treating a patient suffering from sciatica, with no success whatsoever. In desperation this patient turned to Liébeault, who quickly cured him by means of hypnotism. This, to Bernheim, was a professional insult. He knew of Liébeault, thought him a "quack" and decided he would expose this medical menace. So he visited his enemy's clinic—and realized that Liébeault was really a genius. Bernheim immediately began a serious study of hypnotism and for the next twenty years devoted all his great talents to serious work along these lines. His position gave the subject respectable standing and to his eternal honor, he never overlooked an opportunity of directing attention to Liébeault. The latter even sold the remaining copies of his book!

Bernheim realized that the key to hypnotism was suggestion. A doctor, his main interest was along medical lines and his great book *Suggestive Therapeutics* covers this field in great detail. This work stands in a class by itself, only surpassed by the very recent book of Clark L. Hull, Yale University. Hull, as a psychologist has a much wider range of interests than did

Bernheim, so he broadens the field and attacks the problems with modern experimental methods.

Bernheim perfected the "sleeping technique" now so widely used in laboratory practice and described carefully all the phenomena which we have noted in Chapter II of this work.

But animal magnetism, like the cat, proved to have the proverbial nine lives. While Bernheim was doing his great work in Nancy, France, another Frenchman, Charcot, was investigating hypnotism in Paris. Charcot gives us a classic example of what may happen when an authority in one field attempts work in another. One of the world's great anatomists and neurologists, Charcot did pioneer work in these fields which was of the very highest grade. In hypnotism he made about every possible mistake. This is the more amazing because Bernheim, also in France, pointed out these errors as they occurred.

Major hypnotism, as Charcot labelled *his* discovery, showed three sharply marked stages; lethargy, catalepsy and somnambulism. In the first, induced by closing the subject's eyes, he could neither hear nor speak. If now the subject's eyes were opened he—or rather she, for he worked only with women—was still unable to hear or speak. But in this cataleptic stage the limbs would remain in any position in which they were placed. Finally, if the top of the head were rubbed somnambulism was induced. This was practically the same as the trance described by Bernheim.

Many of the results obtained by Charcot were amazing and can be attributed to his complete ignorance of operator attitude. He, as Mesmer one hundred years previously, was convinced that the magnet and the principle of magnetism explained everything. If the subject had a paralysis or a contracture in his right leg, then, if a magnet were brought close to the leg it would immediately shift to the left. More interesting, certain drugs could make their power felt right through a corked bottle. A closed phial of alcohol held near the subject's head would give the proverbial "jag," certainly an inexpensive way of going on a spree.

Bernheim showed that all these curious effects could be produced when they were described in the subject's presence, and it will be recalled that Charcot maintained his subjects were completely deaf in his first two stages. How a man of his scientific skill could have made such a childish slip is difficult to see, but he did. Bernheim produced all Charcot's phenomena by this means, then went a step further. He substituted for the magnet a pencil, a piece of paper or nothing at all, but he got just as good results. In other words, the subject knew what was expected and obliged.

In vain did Bernheim point out to Charcot that the subject in hypnotism is never deaf, is always on the alert for any suggestion. Charcot sailed serenely on. More amazing still is the fact that his great pupil, Alfred Binet, sailed right along with him. Another classic example of how the greatest minds may be blinded by prejudice. For Binet was a great mind, the father of the Binet-Simon test, one of the greatest contributions to psychology, and also the author of *La Suggestibilité,* an original and scientific work. Yet with Féré he published in 1888 his classic book, *Animal Magnetism.* This was no doubt inspired by Bernheim's own work, *Suggestive Therapeutics,* which came off the press two years before. Binet rose in defense of his beloved master, Charcot, running a series of experiments intended to prove beyond any question that Charcot was right.

Hull, who is very impartial on all subjects, writes as follows on this attempt of Binet, "Even so, the fact remains that there has rarely been written a book containing a greater aggregation of results from wretched experiments, all put forward with loud protestations of impeccable scientific procedure and buttressed by the most transparent sophistries, than this work of Binet and Féré."[2] It is curious indeed that two really great men,

---

[2] Clark L. Hull, *Hypnosis and Suggestibility,* p. 16.

Charcot and Binet, could have made such grotesque errors as did these two, even when they invaded a field with which they were unfamiliar.

Bernheim and his "Nancy" school finally laid the ghost of animal magnetism, although every so often we find some operator who is still a follower, at least in part, of Charcot's teaching. One of these is Professor William Brown of Oxford, a psychologist of excellent repute. He does not for one moment support Charcot's crude ideas of magnetism but does follow the "Paris" school in one interesting and rather important detail. Charcot worked only with hysterical women patients, and advanced the theory that hypnotism was a symptom of hysteria. This Bernheim vehemently denied and his views are almost universally accepted.

Nevertheless Brown still holds to this attitude and his opinion is certainly entitled to great respect. The writer, one of Brown's former pupils, feels that he is wrong in this stand. The Oxford psychologist is really a psychiatrist. It is just possible that too much association with mental disease has given Professor Brown a bias in this direction, a tendency to regard everything abnormal as symptomatic of a sick personality; but he still lodges a minority protest. The great majority of psychologists would point out that good hypnotic subjects, as a rule seem to be very normal people. To be sure, cerain signs of dissociation as automatic writing, sleep walking, even hysteria, generally indicate a good subject. But most people who can be put into trance have no such history. Brown would reply that, in these cases, they are "potential" hysterics and the dispute must rest there until we have more evidence.

Bernheim himself made one serious error. He linked hypnotism with sleep, regarding the trance as a special form of normal sleep. As a matter of fact, this is a very natural mistake to make, one into which Pavlov, the great Russian psychologist, also fell. But if the reader cares to look up the experimental evidence on the subject, as set forth by Hull, he will be convinced that sleep and hypnosis have very little in common. The subject is so much "awake" that it would be quite impossible for the reader to detect anything wrong, especially when the subject in question has been coached to act "normal." Moreover, if we test the person in trance, we find that he is quite normal in such things as the conditioned reflex, memory span, psycho-galvanic reflex and other psychological tests.

Confusion here is very easy, especially when the "sleeping" technique is used to induce hypnotism and the subject is not allowed to move about. Actually, many subjects will go into genuine sleep, even snore and lose all touch with the operator. When told to awaken they sleep serenely on, but awaken quite easily if the operator gives them a slight shake. So the mistake of Bernheim, Pavlov and many others was quite natural. We needed the modern experimental laboratory to clear up the fog on this point.

Bernheim was familiar with and described in detail every phenomenon of hypnotism with which we are acquainted at the present day, at least in so far as his times and his interests permitted. Such modern psychological problems as the formation of conditioned reflexes under hypnosis he very naturally does not mention. And he was essentially a doctor, interested in curing patients. Here he was eminently successful. But by the same token he was not interested in the possible uses of hypnotism in education, crime, or warfare. Such problems were completely outside his field. Moreover, practically all of these early authorities, around the close of the nineteenth century, were medical men, their outlook was essentially that of Bernheim, so modern psychology naturally finds many a fascinating problem still unsolved.

Suggestion is undoubtedly the key to hypnotism. However, from the theoretical point of view we are today faced with a very interesting problem. Is it suggestion or dissociation which is really the fundamental cause of hypnosis? Does suggestion cause dissociation as illustrated in automatic writing, speaking with tongues and in all hypnotic phenomena or is it a tendency towards dissociation which makes the good hypnotic subject so suggestible? The writer feels that suggestion is basic. For reasons with which we are not familiar the individual is highly suggestible and dissociation comes as a secondary phenomenon, caused by this peculiarity in personality. But the issue is still open. Also, in so far as we are concerned purely theoretical. We can allow the professional psychologist to ferret out the answer and can proceed with our discussion. We can also leave to him that very vexing problem as to whether all suggestion is really autosuggestion, as Coué maintained.

For our purpose we can say that hypnotism is merely a state of exaggerated suggestibility, induced by artificial means. The vast majority of psychologists would accept this formula, with of course the usual reservations. We do not know what causes suggestibility. Is it acquired or inherited? Does it depend on dissociation or vice versa? We will admit our ignorance and proceed from the assumption that suggestion is the key to hypnosis.

This at once opens other fascinating problems to the general reader. There are other causes of high suggestibility beside hypnosis. These are very evident in our everyday life, in fact they are all important. What is the relation of hypnotism to these other factors? Is it not perhaps possible to explain all with one general formula? Might we not, using hypnotism as a point of departure, be able to understand the phenomenon of Hitler, the basis of mob psychology?

With this end in view the writer advances the theory outlined in the next few pages. Hypnotism is of fascinating interest, but if it has no use outside the psychological laboratory, or in handling the insane it must, of necessity, be of very little practical use to humanity as a whole. But if we can advance a simple working theory which explains both hypnotism and, say, Hitler at one and the same time, then we are being of much greater service to the general public.

In our opinion we can do so and the reader is asked to give

special attention to the following pages of this chapter. The hypothesis we advance is intended to cover the subject in very simple fashion. We purposely avoid many neat psychological questions as being of interest only to the professional psychologist. This leaves us open to the charge of oversimplification but a popular work such as this must view the question "writ large." The details we leave for those round-table discussions wherein men of science delight to go scalp hunting. As a matter of fact the Iroquois raider and the scientist are twin brothers. Scalp hunting is the great national pastime and a very legitimate pastime at that. If the scientist "leads with his chin," he may be perfectly certain that, before many harvest moons have passed he will be defending the old log cabin against the marauding hordes. That is all to the good. It keeps him on his toes and guarantees scientific progress.

The human brain is a very complex photographic plate. The analogy is crude but it will serve as an illustration. Needless to say it is a repeater in the sense that photos are being registered every moment of our waking existence, and by all the various sense organs of sight, hearing, smell, taste, skin senses and others which are more obscure. We, however, are interested in one peculiarity of this plate which is of great importance. It is provided with its own sensitizer. Most of the photographs, the experiences of everyday life are more or less on a dead level. They make a certain impression, we note it and act accordingly, then we probably forget the photo in question for the rest of our natural lives.

Some photographs—experiences—however leave a lasting impression. Five years age we were in an auto crash. Why should we remember that vividly, but not be able to recall anything else for that entire year, at least not recall without an effort. Just common sense! Possibly, but why? We distinctly and vividly recall that at the age of five, or six, or seven we were bitten by a police dog while visiting our uncle's farm. We will have to think in order to recall any other details of that visit. yet the dog experience keeps flashing through our mind even when we don't think. Again it is just common sense but why?

Because at that particular moment the sensitive plate in the brain was vastly more sensitive than at any other time during the whole year. The negative was "over exposed," to draw another analogy from photography and the photo indelibly burned into the plate. Nothing we can do in later life will ever remove that scar. All other experiences of that entire year may become cloudy, may finally disappear completely so far as we are concerned, but every time we see a police dog that old experience of thirty or fifty years ago stands out as vividly as if it were yesterday.

Moreover, as we will see in later chapters, these are just the experiences which really count. They determine our personalities. We could take an entire college course on dogs, could meet all kinds of dogs anywhere. We might even write a book on dogs but we know one thing for certain, we do not like the police dog. Why? Because one bit us fifty years ago. It might just as well have been a collie or a bull, but it wasn't. Logic has nothing to do with the situation. It was a police dog so they are damned in our eyes for all eternity.

It is this type of non-logical, highly emotional reaction which makes the world go round, which leads us into the state of chaos which exists at the present day. For society is essentially a society of human beings which, in many cases, takes its cue from some one leader. Should this leader be unbalanced, overambitious, or a weakling, then all too often his followers will be sacrificed at the altar of his fanaticism or his incompetence.

There are, as far the writer can see, two known devices by which the brain plate can be sensitized. One is hypnotism, the other is emotion. Suggestions given in hypnotism or under emotional strain are carried out with an energy which is quite foreign to normal human conduct. The reader will note that suggestion does not have to be verbal nor recognized as suggestion at the time. Any experience flashing on the mind at such times may act as a suggestion. In hypnotism these are generally by the spoken word, but in everyday life this is far from being the case. The police dog incident was a very strong suggestion. The newspaper is one of the most powerful of suggestive media, especially in a controlled press. But the controlled radio is easily the most potent weapon we have for attaining such ends in our modern civilization.

What has all this to do with hypnotism? Let us take a little excursion into psychology for the next few pages and perhaps we can then see the very close tie-up between hypnotic suggestion and the type of suggestion which is so potent in our daily lives, the suggestion which falls on a brain sensitized by emotion.

The great driving force behind all animal activity is the pleasure-pain principle, the search for pleasure, the avoidance of pain. No normal human being will deliberately step on a tack, unless of course there is a higher pleasure involved. If his child is in danger of being burned to death he may not only step on a tack but get fatally burned himself attempting a rescue. These things are relative. We sit quietly in the dentist's chair and submit willingly (?) to his tortures for we know only too well that if not today, then six months from today he will have us at his mercy. And that six months will not make the ordeal any easier. Also in the human these pleasures may be ideal. Read the tortures which the early Jesuits suffered at the hands of the Indians in *The Bloody Mohawk* by Clarke. It does us modern pampered humans good at times to realize what men will suffer for an ideal. Yet that suffering was in answer to the pleasure principle, weird as the contradiction may seem to the average of humanity.

This pleasure principle has its basis in the instinct. In view of the fact that the word instinct is unpopular in scientific circles these days the reader may think in terms of drives or impulses if he chooses. Psychology has officially thrown instinct out the front door, then given it a new name and welcomed it in by the kitchen entrance. The writer prefers the word instinct and will use it in spite of its black name in psychological circles.

These instincts are almost always of such a nature that they

aid in survival of the species, but not necessarily of the individual. Pleasure is the reward which the animal receives for
carrying out the instinct, pain is the red light, the warning not
to repeat the offense in the future.

Moreover, since these instincts are basic, are the foundations
on which a species survives or is exterminated, it is very important that they be reinforced. Closely tied up with these various instincts we have certain emotions, such as fear, rage or
love, and these emotions together with their attendant feelings
of pleasure or the opposite sensitize the brain. Thus experiences
which directly arouse our instincts tend to make a greater impression on the brain plate, to be remembered better, as we say.
We can look on them as suggestions.

Finally, just a word as to intelligence. It was long the custom
to contrast instinct and intelligence. Instinct represented the
baser side of man, whereas intelligence was something on a
much higher plane, the pure and noble side of man's nature.
Actually intelligence is the servant of the instinct, of the pleasure
principle. We use our intelligence to gratify our search for
pleasure, be these pleasures low or idealistic. We may reason
with a child for days to no effect. We may tell little Johnny
that he is not to play with strange dogs, and he is unimpressed.
Let one of those same dogs take a nip at him and he has
learned his lesson. That one experience, falling on a brain
sensitized by fear, will leave a lasting impression. It is "burned
in" so to speak.

Hypnotism and emotion, be that emotion pleasurable or the
opposite, are the only forces which we are certain have this
effect on the photographic plate of the brain. It seems possible
that certain drugs, such as alcohol may under certain circumstances, produce the same results, but we are not certain. It is
highly probable that hypnotism in its turn depends on emotion.
Ferenczi, a psychoanalyst, has given a formula which may very
easily express the situation. He says, "Suggestion depends on
transference and transference is a shifting of the libido."

In plainer English, his theory runs somewhat along these

lines. In hypnotism the operator takes the place of the subject's parent, father or mother. The subject transfers to the hypnotist the feeling he had for this parent as a child. The attitude of the operator in question will determine whether he is to be father or mother. If the subject, as a child, was submissive to this parent, he will be a good hypnotic subject and vice versa. This attitude of the child is obviously one of emotion, so that hypnotism, according to Ferenczi, would depend on emotion. A neat theory which may or may not be true. The writer is inclined to favor it.

Be that as it may, we can now perhaps see a little more clearly how the laws of hypnotism may become so very important in our everyday life. Every situation we face in life is a social situation, that is to say it involves other people. Almost invariably this situation involves a leader. He may be appointed, he may seize authority, or he may just gravitate to the top. The boss in the office is a typical example, the dictator on the radio not so typical but far more powerful. Now if by any device this leader can arouse our emotions, can "get under our skins," then his words, his suggestions, falling on our sensitized brains will have far more weight than those same suggestions given us by a stranger or in a magazine article where no emotion is involved. He is, to all intents and purposes, a hypnotist.

Our reactions may be antagonistic—negative suggestion— but we will react violently. But if the dictator or boss in question knows his business he will take care that they do not arouse antagonism. He will appeal to the pleasure principle in some form or other. He will tell us that we are being persecuted, robbed, hemmed in. He will appeal to our patriotism, our love of home and family. He will promise us security, wealth, glory if we but do as he says. And if he knows what he is about we will fall under his spell just as surely as a subject ever falls under the trance of a hypnotist.

This technique of "direct" or "prestige" suggestion we see clearly in the stage hypnotist. His success depends on a forceful, frontal attack. He never allows the subject's gaze to shift from his own and literally bullies him into the hypnotic trance. Here we have clear evidence of the emotional factor in hypnosis. The psychologist in his laboratory also uses this prestige suggestion although in a quieter form. But whether it be the stage hypnotist, the laboratory psychologist or Hitler on the radio results are the same, so far as psychology is concerned. The suggestions fall on a highly sensitized brain and such suggestions have tremendous force, a force altogether out of proportion to any value that the proposals, as such, may have.

Let us now consider a few facts which we have gathered from our study of hypnotism in the laboratory. One in every five of the human race are highly suggestible, at least half are suggestible to a very considerable degree. But here mere figures do not tell the story. That one-fifth has a power far beyond its numbers, for this type of man, acting under direct suggestion, is no mere average person. He is a fanatic in the highest—or lowest—sense of the word.

The writer several years ago had a very unpleasant experience which illustrates the point. He wished to show the power of the posthypnotic suggestion so he suggested to Smith that, on awakening he would go over and insist on sitting in Brown's chair. Smith and Brown were relative strangers. When he was awakened, Smith paused a moment, then got up and walked over to Brown.

"Mind if I sit in your chair?"

"Yes. I like the chair myself."

Without a word Smith reached down, took Brown by the shoulder, and literally hurled him across the room. Then he sat down, muttering savagely that if Brown so much as opened his mouth he'd send him through the window as well. And he meant just that. A few such experiences teach the operator to "take it easy." On another occasion the writer suggested to a subject in hypnotism that an individual he particularly disliked was standing in front of the door. Without an instant's hesitation the subject strode up to the door and drove his fist through the panel. The individual who is highly suggestible, whether from hypnotism or from strong emotion, reacts with a passionate fury which leaves us other mere mortals staring in open-eyed wonder. But it is terribly real, as Europe can testify today.

There is still another line of approach which shows us the very close relation between the suggestibility of hypnotism and that arising from the emotions. Basic to psychoanalysis, as outlined by Freud, is the so-called complex. Freud discovered that many of our early childhood experiences are forgotten in a curious sort of way. The forgetting is not passive but active; they do not just fade away into oblivion, they are literally thrown out of consciousness, they are "repressed" into the unconscious.

Such experiences are always unpleasant in nature and are forced out of consciousness in accord with the pleasure principle we have already stressed. Not only will the body not undergo pain willingly, unless for a future pleasure, but the mind also turns away from painful thoughts. The reader can easily think of exceptions, but we would again warn that many apparent exceptions are not real. A person may brood over bad treatment, which is unpleasant, but this in turn may bring up the feeling of self-pity which is very pleasant. Or he may plan revenge, thinking out various ways in which he will even up the score. This also may be pleasant.

Actually, however, the pleasure principle does not work in nearly as clear cut form in the mind as in the body. To a great degree we lose the power of repression after the age of five, although under great stress, as in war, it may still act very effectively. But it does work in childhood and Freud discovered that many of the neuroses have their origin in these repressions. They are "down" but not "out." Why they are not out is beside our discussion here, but once they become installed in the unconscious they can cause a lot of trouble.

For example, a child is badly frightened by a cat. Later in

life he develops a fear, a phobia of cats. Yet strange to say the original experience in which he was frightened has been completely forgotten. Note the close resemblance to the posthypnotic suggestion. All we need is the hypnotist, rather than the cat, to give the suggestion and the parallel would be complete.

These complexes act in very curious fashion. We can tell what causes them but we cannot predict results. A little boy was going to the store. He had to pass through a narrow alley way closed at both ends by a door. He got into the alley, the door behind him snapped shut, the door in front was closed. Then he found there was a dog in the alley as well, which promptly attacked him. This frightened the child very badly. In later life this incident was forgotten, repressed, but the complex did its work. Strange to say, however, he did not develop a fear of dogs, as one would have expected, but a fear of closed spaces—claustrophobia. His main idea was to get out of that closed alley. This was the autosuggestion which, given in a state of great emotion, later came out as a complex—a posthypnotic suggestion.

Another little boy was sliding down hill. His sled collided with a fence and his hand was badly cut. The doctor could not give him an anaesthetic, but had to sew up the hand while he was wide awake, a very painful and terrifying experience. This was repressed and later came out, not as a fear of doctors, but a fear of black bags. The doctor had with him a black bag and the eyes of the child were riveted on this bag, for from here the doctor took the instruments which caused him so much pain.

This particular type of posthypnotic suggestion may come out in various ways, but the complex is, to all intents and purposes, a posthypnotic suggestion. Fright by a cat may appear in later life as a fear of cats. But it may just as easily come out in the form of a compulsion to kill cats. The writer had a friend who got himself in no end of trouble with his neighbors because of this. Or again it may appear as an obsession that people are looking at him with cat's eyes. This may become so strong that the individual may be very dangerous, even murdering his supposed persecutor.

But note again the very close tie-up between the complex and the posthypnotic suggestion. The complex, we know, is definitely caused by strong unpleasant emotion. Moreover, it works along almost identical lines with the posthypnotic suggestion. Not quite as specific, to be sure, but just as compulsive. Also we would find the other characteristic of the posthypnotic suggestion present if we cared to look, namely rationalization.

So here again we see that emotion and hypnotism seem to sensitize the brain in identical fashion. The suggestion which is given in either case leaves an indelible impression and provokes to acts which are quite apart from any intellectual processes the individual may use.

We may summarize the last few pages somewhat as follows. Suggestibility, present in all people to a greater or less degree, is very marked in certain individuals. This appears due to the fact that their brains can be very easily sensitized to "photographs"—experiences—either by hypnotism or by emotion. We do not know whether the hypnotic subject is always the one who in adult life is open to emotional sensitization, for no great amount of investigation has been done on this question. It does seem highly probable that hypnotism is closely linked to emotion, and these two types of brain sensitization are essentially one and the same.

Hence comes the great importance of hypnotism as a "laboratory" in which to study this whole problem of suggestibility, for the phenomena of suggestion are tremendously important. Around this question centers the whole problem of mob psychology, the psychology of such leaders as Hitler. Without in any way juggling words we can truthfully say that he was one of the greatest hypnotists of all time. Yet he may never have heard of the subject. We will return to this in the later chapters of the book.

Chapter VI

MEDICAL USES OF HYPNOTISM

THE sanity of insanity. Strange as it may seem the man or woman whom we class as insane is, in one respect, far more sane than we. The great quest of man is happiness—the pursuit of the pleasure principle. As a group the insane are the happiest of all people. To be sure, there are exceptions, especially among the "organic" or "structural" insanities—psychoses—where the brain is actually damaged by syphilis, brain tumor or bursting blood vessels. But the "functional" insane, those in whom the brain is in no way diseased, have realized the full truth of the words when wrongly interpreted, "The kingdom of God is within you." These people have learned that they can retreat into a life of daydreams, cut off all contact with reality, and be happy ever afterward. Napoleon in the asylum *is* Napoleon. To be sure, the French Government would not agree, but he will present you with the province of Normandy or with French Indo-China as a gift, if he happens to like the cut of your nose. Further, he absolutely believes that he can do so. To be sure he has to explain why he, Napoleon, is in the asylum. But that is easy. He is a great man persecuted by his enemies. Soon he will be free and then—ah then—just watch what he does to the President of France for his low tricks.

We can understand Napoleon fairly well if we understand the psychology of suggestion. He is fairly typical of these functional psychoses, the most numerous of all the insane. Some will be more degenerated than he as regards intelligence, some others will substitute bodily actions for his grandiose ideas but, by and large, the picture is the same. An individual who has retreated from reality in following the pleasure principle. And this we can best explain by the laws of suggestion.

Let us take an example. Little Johnny, as a boy, is much like other boys but not quite as husky. He does not like the rough and tumble of his street, with its accompaniment of black eyes and bloody noses. So he tends to withdraw from the group and live with his books and pictures. But he still craves power and recognition, as do all of us. Then, in some such cases, he makes a very splendid discovery. If he just imagines hard enough, he can have a lot of fun from building castles in the air. In his own mind he becomes a great inventor and likes to picture himself as a new edition of Edison or Steinmetz. He overlooks the fact that such geniuses climbed the ladder by facing, not retreating from, reality. The blistered hands and long hours of hard mental work which were their preparation he neglects completely. He retreats more and more into his life of daydreams until this becomes the only real life so far as he is concerned.

Then as a young man, he snaps the last bond. He discovers that in the moon is a great dynamo of energy which is subject to his will. He can direct it in any way he wishes, either to destroy this world or convert it into a modern Utopia. He explains his ideas to his friends, may write the President of the United States about it, even threaten him with destruction if he does not "play ball." Most do not go to this extreme but whether they do or not their friends realize there is something wrong, get in touch with the authorities, and next they arrive in the asylum, probably for the duration of their natural lives.

Let us see exactly how suggestion, of which hypnotism is only an exaggerated form, explains such a case. Emotion sensitizes the brain and these daydreams are very pleasant. Every time he dwells upon them the photo plate—to use this crude analogy—of the mind is highly receptive. They become "burned in," as it were. Moreover, since they are pleasant, he is following the pleasure principle when he daydreams on every possible occasion. The whole thing slowly becomes a closed and vicious circle. His thoughts become more and more centered around these ideas, until they cannot escape from that orbit even if they would. At this point he loses all contact with reality and we say he is insane.

We get this picture very clearly when we talk to these people in the asylum. Their minds are far, far away. They are "absent minded" to the most extreme degree. Now and then we can establish contact and for a minute or two they seem perfectly sane. Then again they are off on their delusions, describing to us how their insides are of solid gold. Finally they give up even talking to us and retreat again into their very pleasant thoughts.

Hypnotism—or suggestion—can explain such cases but cannot effect a cure. Suggestion has already done its work. They have arrived at their goal of happiness and actively resist any attempt at cure. After all, this is quite reasonable. They have spent ten, twenty, thirty years building up this beautiful dream palace and along comes a silly doctor who wants to tear it down over night. Their answer is an emphatic "no." So the reader must bear in mind that while, in many cases we can explain accurately why a patient is insane, and that while this insanity may be due to suggestion, nevertheless we are quite helpless in effecting a cure by hypnotism.

In cases such as those quoted above, the patient is now suggestible in the wrong direction. He is "negatively" suggestible. For example, we may take one of these cases of dementia praecox or schizophrenia, as it is called, stand him up in front of us and say "Sit down." He remains standing.

Then we say, "Very well, stand where you are." He promptly sits.

We say, "That's fine. Now just sit there while I take your blood pressure." He immediately stands up.

In other words he has arrived at his goal of happiness. He senses that the doctor in question wishes to tear down his dream palace, so in defense he does exactly the opposite of any request. From his point of view this makes good sense, but certainly does not help toward a cure. Most of the insane are so unco-operative that it is quite impossible to induce hypnotism even to a slight degree.

However, there are a great many people whom the layman would say are insane or at least "queer", whom the psychologist would call neurotic. The subject is still in touch with reality, he is living in a real world, even if he is very poorly adjusted to the same. Here we would class the hysteric.

We explain the hysterical individual by saying that he or she is a grown-up five year old. We can explain it again on the basis of the pleasure principle, the pleasures of a child. The hysteric has an intense longing for attention, for sympathy. He does not realize that the proper way to get this attention is by hard work and real accomplishment. As a child he learns that he can become the center of attention if he lies on the floor, kicks and screams. This works so well that as an adult he does the same, and we say he has an attack of convulsions.

There are all kinds of hysterical symptoms besides these convulsions, such as attacks of weeping, paralysis of an arm or a leg, even hysterical blindness or deafness. These can all be explained on the basis of autosuggestion. The patient finds it very pleasant to be the center of attention. This sensitizes the brain, so each time he repeats the hysterical "attack" that line of conduct becomes more deeply burned into the brain plate. He repeats as often as possible because of the pleasure involved, so we again have that vicious circle.

But the hysteric lives in a real world. He does not retreat from reality, so much as he manipulates reality. He still lives with his family but he uses all his tricks to make its members his slaves. He learns that the very best device with which to center attention on himself is to be sick, hence the endless list of pains, convulsions, indigestion, "heart" attacks and so forth with which the hysteric dominates his world.

Now, strange to say, this type of person is very easily hypnotized, so much so that William Brown claims hypnotism to be a symptom of hysteria. We have already noted our disagreement with this point of view. But here again, while the patient is easily hypnotized, and while hysteria is caused by suggestion, it is very difficult to effect a cure by the same means. And for the same reason as insanity proper. The patient has spent all his life pursuing the pleasure principle toward the goal of hysteria. He is an hysteric by choice, not by compulsion. The choice may be one of the unconscious mind, and the patient may deny indignantly that he wishes to be sick, but psychology now realizes that the unconscious mind is quite as important as the conscious, at least in this matter of mental health.

So the hysteric actively resists cure but at the same time wants to be cured, strange as that may seem. Consciously he insists that he will co-operate but it is always the proverbial way to hell paved with good intentions. He cheerfully co-operates in any line of treatment and is delighted to find it doesn't work. He, of all people, enjoys being sick.

Yet he is very suggestible and hypnotism in many cases can produce a cure, more or less by the "strong arm" method. We have already pointed out the tremendously compulsive power of the posthypnotic suggestion. If now, in hypnotism, we point out to the patient the pleasure he will get from being well and healthy, the pleasure it will give his family, and above all things, the added esteem he will have from all his friends, we may be able by the sheer force of suggestion to swing the pleasure principle into new channels.

But these cases are notoriously unstable. Grown-up five-year-olds, they use their pains and aches to get the sympathy and attention they crave. If this attention is not forthcoming under the new line of treatment they are always liable to "back slide." They have never faced reality on the adult level, which is a pretty difficult task even for well adjusted people in this year of 1943. The slightest discouragement or reverse and they are

right back where they started from. Yet in some cases hypnotism, carefully used, works wonders. The reader is referred to
Bernheim's book *Suggestive Therapeutics* for a very careful
discussion of many hysterical cases.

The psychoanalyst has noted this weakness in the hysteric
and has pointed out the fact that hypnotism is not always successful. There is a tendency for the hysterical symptom, when
cured, to return in another form, because of the basic weakness
in the patient, his search for attention and sympathy on the
five-year-old level. The psychoanalyst explains hysteria by the
complex, which we have already mentioned. In his opinion the
only way to cure hysteria is to search out this complex and
bring it back to consciousness—the process of reintegration.
The patient will then realize just what is causing the trouble
and will cure himself.

But the psychologist is always suspicious of the psychoanalyst
in his blasts against hypnotism. To quote a well known passage,
"The lady protests too much, methinks." More than one article
has been written pointing out the great effect with which the
psychoanalyst uses suggestion, generally without the slightest
intention of so doing. It is the old problem of "operator attitude." The psychoanalyst tends to react to these charges with
much too vehement denials. Instead of admitting the uses of
suggestion he tends rather to adopt the other extreme of complete denial, at least in so far as his own technique is concerned.

The truth probably lies somewhere between the assertions
of both camps. The hysteric is notoriously difficult to handle,
because of that tendency to backslide—to regress in the psychoanalytic language. Hypnotism has certainly affected some
striking cures, unless Bernheim and his followers were completely mistaken. That is hardly possible. On the other hand
psychoanalysis has also had some very startling successes. It
would seem that we can, at present, only say that both are
useful. To wholeheartedly condemn one or the other is to fly
in the face of our evidence. A cure by either method would seem

to depend on the patient himself, his co-operation, the duration of the trouble and the strength of his whole personality in the matter of facing reality.

When we shift to the other so-called psychoneuroses the picture is distinctly different. Here we have the phobias—fears—the compulsion and the obsessions. For example, let us consider the hand-washing compulsion, previously mentioned. Here the patient must wash his hands forty times a day. This condition can become terribly exasperating. One patient fought against the compulsion furiously and finally solved the problem in drastic fashion. He put one hand on a block and hewed it off with an ax. The other he thrust under a rotary saw. That ended the compulsion—and the sufferer.

In these psychoneuroses it would seem that the symptoms are no longer directed by the pleasure principle. The patient does not enjoy washing his hands, neither does he enjoy his fear of cats or his obsession that everyone is looking at him. Quite the contrary, for he does everything he can to resist, but to no avail. With kleptomania, the morbid compulsion to steal, for example, the patient has a compulsion to steal which cannot be resisted even if a policeman is at his shoulder. Yet, strange to say, the theft is often of worthless articles which the individual could easily afford to buy. The book by Healy *Mental Conflicts and Misconduct* gives a very good picture of the state.

Here, it would seem to the writer we have another condition caused by suggestion. The patient, as a child, is badly frightened by, let us say, a cat. This experience falling on the brain sensitized by fear gives us the suggestion, which later turns up as a posthypnotic suggestion, the phobia of cats. Yet, strange to say, while we know the cause it is very difficult to apply the cure. The reason seems to be largely the time element. The picture is so deeply burned into the brain plate with the passing of the years that no amount of counter suggestion in hypnotism can erase the same. Healy gives us a very useful rule of thumb. If we can treat such a patient before the age of twelve, we will probably have success, but if we begin such treatment after that age we will likely fail.

That rule, of course, is by no means hard and fast, but it does emphasize a very important fact about all mental disease. Time is a very important factor. Unless the compulsion, phobia, tendency to hysteria or to dementia praecox is checked very early, it tends to take on the nature of a habit. This does not make a cure impossible but it does make one much more difficult. We see this very well illustrated in the new type of treatment used for dementia praecox, namely insulin shock. Here we have very good success if only the patient is taken early. If treatment is given within the first two years the rate of cure—remission is a better word—is about eighty per cent. Then it drops off very sharply and it would appear that insulin is not of much use with older sufferers. There are the usual exceptions but such seems to be the rule.

To the average reader insanity is just insanity and he tends to label all people who are a little odd as being also a little "crazy." But the psychologist is very particular about his word. First of all he does not use the terms "insane" or "crazy" at all. They are social definitions, they are more or less utilitarian in view. Is the individual a menace to society? If so, then he is insane and away with him. If not, he is sane so we allow him his liberty.

The psychologist looks at things somewhat differently. The man who has a compulsion to wash his hands forty times a day is just as ill mentally as the man with a compulsion to cut the ears off every red headed man he sees. One is quite safe to have at large, the other is very dangerous. The individual who must touch every other lamp-post is no menace to society but the man who must set fires, the pyromaniac, may very easily land in the penitentiary. Yet they are both equally ill from the mental viewpoint.

The really "insane" we term psychotics, although our law courts would put others in this group. The psychoses we divide into the structural and the functional. In the former the brain itself is injured by syphilis, tumor, bursting blood vessel, hardening of the arteries. Here it would seem natural to suppose that hypnotism can be of no use.

We would expect something better, however, when we come to the "functional" psychoses. There is nothing wrong with the brain. If we examine, after his death, the brain of a patient with dementia praecox or manic depressive insanity we find his brain is quite as good as our own. It is a "habit" psychosis; he has learned the wrong habits of thought. He has pursued the pleasure principle up the "wrong alley," so to speak, the street which leads to the asylum. Yet we can do almost nothing with him for he is happy in his insanity. His condition is his own choice. Not only, as a rule, can we not hypnotize him but he is negatively suggestible. He does just the opposite from what we wish.

Hysteria we would class as a psychoneurosis. The subject is in touch with reality. He is still living in a real world, as opposed to the psychotic, but in an unreal fashion. A grown-up child, he uses childish devices to center sympathy on himself. Generally the hysteric is a good hypnotic subject so we would hope for a high rate of cure in these cases. And such is the picture we get, but unfortunately these cures tend to be very temporary. The hysteric is the world's worst "backslider." Basic to the picture is that childish personality which cannot face reality, which seeks pleasure on the five-year-level. With time and great patience we may persuade the patient to grow up and "act his age," but he needs constant supervision.

The compulsions, phobias and obsessions we also class as psychoneurotics. Here the patient is also living in a real world and we have a distinct advantage in dealing with him. He actually wants to get well. He doesn't enjoy being sick, being afraid of cats, having to set fires or being obsessed with the idea that he is being poisoned. So we can generally count on real co-operation, not the lip service we expect from the hysteric.

If the reader would review the literature he would find that hypnotism was fairly successful in handling these cases, but again much depends on the time factor. If the case is not of long standing, that is to say if we begin treatment before the age of twelve, the outlook is good; if not, it may be bad. But even here success will depend on so many intangibles, especially the nature of the original "hypnotic" trance on which this "posthypnotic" suggestion is based. This is exactly what we would expect from our knowledge of hypnotism. Some people, even if fairly good subjects can resist the posthypnotic suggestion very nicely, others cannot. And these neurotic symptoms are essentially posthypnotic suggestions.

The world has heard a great deal of psychoanalysis. We have already pointed out that, according to this school, many human ills are caused by childish and very unpleasant experiences being "repressed," forced into the unconscious, and that these so-called complexes act in almost identical fashion to the post-hypnotic suggestion. The cure in psychoanalysis is accomplished when these forgotten experiences are dragged out of the unconscious into the conscious mind. The subject then remembers the childhood incident, reacts to it as an adult and it loses its power. To accomplish this end the psychoanalyst uses two main devices, free association and dream analysis.

There can be no doubt that the complex is a very real thing and that it does cause a great deal of trouble in adult life, even as the psychoanalysts claim. We would expect this from our knowledge of the posthypnotic suggestion. Also we agree that it should be brought to the surface and "reintegrated" with the conscious mind. We know that the subject in hypnotism can resist the posthypnotic suggestion much easier if he remembers the suggestion having been given. All this makes very good sense.

So the psychologist proposes the use of hypno-analysis and the psycho-analyst immediately objects. With the use of hypnotism we can explore the unconscious mind very quickly and effectively, often recovering these lost childhood memories in a fraction of the time taken by the psychoanalyst. We can then have the subject remember these experiences when awake, and we have accomplished our end.

By the way, it may interest the reader to know some of the curious things which happen when we insist on the subject remembering very unpleasant experiences. In cases of shell shock we have already mentioned that the patient has generally forgotten some very horrible occurrence. It has been thrown out of consciousness and, lodged in the unconscious, it is responsible for the various symptoms. The first move is to recover this memory. So we hypnotize the patient, have him describe just what happened in the trance state, then tell him he will remember it on awakening. We wake him up and find that he still has no memory of the incident.

We re-hypnotize him and return to the attack. We again have him describe the scene and again insist that he must remember this when he is awake. Then we again awaken him—only we don't. He refuses to wake up. That is his way of protecting himself. But in the long run, by sheer insistence, we generally succeed in getting the experience once more back in consciousness. Curiously enough, it does no good to describe the occurrence to him. We can do so in the greatest detail, assuring him that it actually happened to him twenty-four hours back. It is just the same as some one telling us what we did when we were "out on our feet" from a blow or from a drug, let us say alcohol.

Hypno-analysis is slowly coming into its own. The psychoanalyst opposes it for reasons which seem wholly inadequate. We suspect, as we have already indicated, that it is a guilty conscience. Hypnotism explains so much of psychoanalysis, especially the nature of the complex, that the psychoanalyst here is afraid to use hypnotism for fear the tail will begin to wag the dog. Yet he cannot get away from the fact that it is a tremendous time saver and, if psychoanalysis is ever to be in general use, something must be done. The time used is tremendous. At least three hundred hours with the analyst. When we remember that the high grade practitioner will charge twenty-five dollars an hour for his time we can well appreciate the weight of Freud's statement "Psychoanalysis is not for the poor."

Outside this realm of the "insane" and the "queer" there are other branches of medicine where hypnotism has a possible use. This is especially so along the lines of so-called bad habits. For example, let us consider the problem of the pervert, the individual whose sex life takes some outlet generally disapproved by society. This outlet is often toward the same sex, giving us the typical homosexual.

Here we run into exactly the same problem we do in the case of the hysteric. The sex life is on a very immature level and the individual follows his line of action because of the pleasure principle. The pervert, in general, does not want to be cured. He is quite happy as he is, so we may count on very little co-operation, even as with the hysteric. Lip service, to be sure. Plenty of assurance that he or she will do everything possible to "reform," but experience soon teaches the operator to place very little reliance on these protestations.

However, the subject does have one real advantage, which may not appear so to him. He is where he is because of the pleasure principle. But he is living in a very real world and the hand of society may fall with brutal force on the pervert, much more so than on any of the cases so far mentioned. The results may be very unpleasant, so unpleasant in fact that they will outweigh the immature pleasure drive which is the cause of his trouble. In this case he may give the doctor genuine co-operation when he seeks a cure.

Even so, results are none too hopeful. Rarely indeed does the homosexual succeed in readjusting to a normal sex life. The reason is the same as with the hysteric. The pleasure principle has lead him where he is and, frankly, he is quite satisfied with life—unless he crosses the law. The psychoanalyst would say there is a weak spot in his personality synthesis. Instead of developing into a normal adult, facing adult reality, he became arrested—fixated—at an earlier stage of development. A more simple explanation would be in terms of suggestion. Seduced at an early age, this experience—suggestion—made such an imprint on the sensitized brain plate that it cannot be removed. In as much as the resulting activity is pleasant, he does not try seriously to fight the trend but accepts it. There will always be this weakness with the constant danger of a backslip into the perversion.

The reader may easily get the idea that hypnotism is not of much use in the treatment of mental disease. As a matter of fact it is—as much as anything. Neurotic states are notoriously difficult to handle by *any* method. There is a fundamental personality weakness basic to all these patients, a weakness dating generally to childhood, acting with all the power of the post-hypnotic suggestion and which has probably been accepted for twenty or thirty years. It is extremely hard to remake the personality after such an experience. The time element alone is a great factor in mental disease—and generally the psychiatrist does not see his patient until the condition is hopelessly "burned in." One authority says "the neurotic is remarkably consistent in his inconsistency." He will make all sorts of promises to reform, may really mean to do so—at the moment. Twenty-four hours later there is great danger that he will again be faced with his old trouble.

We can claim that hypnotism is as successful as any other attack in this very difficult field. We would have to make an exception in the insulin and cardiazol treatment of dementia praecox which is producing such startling results. But compare hypnotism with psychoanalysis or any other standard treatment for mental disease and results will be favorable. In the great majority of cases the condition is quite incurable by any means. Hypnotism, where it can be used, is in our opinion the best form of attack. At least we can begin with this. If we fail, we can resort to other methods. One great advantage of hypnotism is that results are quick and relatively clear-cut. You do or you don't! By the end of twenty-four hours we can either say that we are making definite progress or that we are getting nowhere. This is a great advantage.

We cannot be too encouraging on this subject of the neuroses and psychoses. They are difficult to deal with by *any* method. For a very sane discussion of the use of hypnotism in this field see the book by O. Diethelm, *Treatment in Psychiatry*. But we can very definitely get results in many cases of so-called bad habits. Alcoholism is an excellent example and for a much more detailed discussion than we give in the next few paragraphs we refer the reader to *The Psychology of Alcoholism,* by G. B. Cutten.

Here we can use the posthypnotic suggestion with devastating and often humorous effect. It is simply an endurance game and should the patient be a good hypnotic subject the operator holds all the aces. The attack is based on that curious control which hypnotism gives us over the autonomic nervous system and through it the organs of the body. We suggest that the subject in future will be deathly sick to his stomach every time he touches alcohol, that the taste will be bad and that he will vomit. We may have to return to the attack several times but with a good subject we will probably succeed. Once we get this posthypnotic suggestion working it is only a matter of time. No human being will get much pleasure from liquor if the very smell of it makes him vomit. He cannot even keep it on his stomach long enough to register a "jag."

The reader will please note, however, that the problem is not quite that simple. Alcoholism is not a disease, it is a symptom of a diseased personality, of one which cannot face reality and chooses the relaxation supplied by liquor as a way out, a retreat. So we must strengthen the personality or, having ejected one devil we may find seven others in its place. The others in this case, may be drugs and the last state will be much worse than the first.

So we do everything in our power to make the individual face reality, and also to supply an "out" which meets with social approval. This substitute retreat may take one of many forms, depending on the nature of the case. Religion is excellent, but we have to discover, if possible, some natural liking of the individual which can be used. Then we try to make the patient just as much an addict to, say, chess, as he was to alcohol. All sorts of hobbies can be used to take the place of alcohol, but always we must bear in mind that the individual really must have some retreat and this retreat must be one which will not cause trouble. One patient became such a chess fan that he would wake up at 2 A.M. and spend the rest of the night doing problems. Not a very desirable situation perhaps, but certainly better than reaching for a bottle.

We must never take the alcoholic for granted. Always in the back of his mind will be the longing for some substitute which may take the place of liquor. The great danger is drugs and any move in this direction is very certainly one from the proverbial frying pan into the fire. Hypnotism supplies us with a very effective weapon against alcoholism and illustrates neatly the psychoanalysts great criticism of hypnotism. The doctor cures the "symptom" and calls it a day, overlooking the fact that alcoholism is merely a symptom, a sign of much more serious trouble. Block the outlet here and we may very easily have a much worse "symptom" with which to deal.

Hypnotism seems to lend itself also to the treatment of excessive smoking and by much the same technique as that advocated for its use to combat alcohol. Here, of course, the condition is by no means as serious and the treatment appears to be much easier.

But, strange as it may seem, hypnotism is of very little use in the treatment of drugs such as morphine, cocaine or hashish. The public tends to confuse the action and nature of these drugs with alcohol, but in reality they are totally different. Alcohol is not a "habit former," in and of itself. It simply provides an escape from the care and worries of this life, little more. If we can substitute another escape the individual will accept this, and in the long run will find it quite as satisfactory as was alcohol.

Morphine, as an example of the other group, acts in quite different fashion. To be sure, the individual generally starts "dope" as an escape. The feeling of peace and relaxation which comes from morphine compares very favorably with that obtained from alcohol. But once the individual has obtained the morphine habit, is an "addict," then morphine and only morphine or some other derivative of opium will satisfy the craving. And this craving is a craving of the *body itself*, is physiological, as we say. The body demands and literally must have the drug in question.

This is well seen in the so-called tolerance which the body builds for the drug, something quite foreign to alcohol. For example, if we should take the average reader and give him by hypodermic syringe one half grain of morphine, results might be serious. One grain would probably cause death. But if that same reader became an addict, then in a year's time he could safely take fifty grains a day. One hundred grains is quite common with addicts and even daily doses of two hundred fifty grains by no means unknown!

Now suppose we wish to "cure" the individual in question. We put him in a sanitarium and take away the drug completely. We at once have a very sick man on our hands. The "withdrawal" symptoms may be so severe as to cause death. As a result the withdrawal of the drug has to be under very careful medical supervision. Even after the subject is "off" the drug the danger of a return is very great. There is always that constant craving for morphine which can only be met by one particular brand of drugs, the opium group.

This picture is quite different from that given by alcohol or tobacco. The body builds little, if any tolerance and there are no withdrawal symptoms. We can take an alcoholic and cut off all his liquor tomorrow. We will have a very unhappy individual on our hands but he is not physically sick; certainly there is no danger of death. But with these other drugs the craving for the specific "dope" is quite different.

We know definitely that three drug groups act in this fashion. Opium and all its derivatives as morphine, codeine, heroin is perhaps the best known. Cocaine and its relatives are equally dangerous, while marihuana—the American version of hashish —is only lately becoming known in this country. Hypnotism can do very little against these. It can strengthen the will power, the determination to resist, but the subject will literally go through hell for the drug in question. We can suggest vomiting and will succeed but it means nothing. The counter drive is far too strong to be counteracted by the fear of a sick stomach.

It would seem that there would be a fertile field for hypnotism in the bad character habits of childhood. Bad sex practices naturally occur to us in this respect but there are many others. The tendency to truancy, to bad temper, to stealing, even to actual crime. We must bear in mind here that the child is far more suggestible than is the adult. Bernheim found that about four fifths of children after the age of seven could be thrown into somnambulism. Very recent work such as that by Reymert and Kohn would seem to uphold this claim. So we may safely say that the child in general is a much better subject than is the adult.

We must also remember that time is very much of a factor in the establishment of all these bad "habits." Healy gives us a rule of thumb with reference to kleptomania, the compulsion to steal. If we attack the problem before the age of twelve, we will probably succeed, but if after this age we are probably faced with failure. Very little work has been done in this field and it is no fault of the doctor. Blind prejudice on the public's side is so strong that any medical man or educator who dares use hypnotism to cure the bad habits of childhood is immediately placed in the ranks of the quacks and charlatans. Humanity is curiously and wonderfully made. We will gladly have our children listen to Hitler or any other high power orator over the radio while he uses suggestion to warp their judgments. But if the doctor or educator should use identical suggestions on these children with the aid of hypnotism he would be due for a coat of tar and feathers.

Some day, perhaps fifty or one hundred fifty years from today, our descendants will look back at us with the same curiosity and wonder with which we regard our own ancestors of a while back. Pasteur was held up to ridicule when he asserted that the germ might cause disease. Vesalius was almost burned at the stake when he dared cut up the human body to get some knowledge of anatomy. One hundred years from now the scientist will be amused at the strange ignorance which banned the use of hypnotism in the formation of youthful character and the correction of "nervous" ailments.

For example, the writer once listened to an excellent paper on stammering by a well known authority read before a medical society. Following this paper the writer asked the author if he had ever tried hypnotism in the treatment of speech disorders. The let down was terrific. The speaker looked confused, then embarrassed. How was he to be courteous and answer such a silly question? He was obviously puzzled to find that any member of a self respecting medical organization could "lead with his chin" in such childish fashion. But he displayed the usual tact which is so characteristic of the medical profession and passed the question off much as the reader would pass off a child's question about black magic or fairies.

Yet, hypnotism is a well recognized means of attacking speech defects in Europe. Not a sure cure, by any means. Those of us who have tried to handle cases of stammering know how extremely resistant to treatment this condition may be. We do not even know what causes it. There are seven good theories and probably seventeen more that are not so good. Moreover we can cure some cases with everything from the gypsy's thread around the finger to psychoanalysis. Some others seem absolutely incurable.

Hypnotism has its list of cures and also its list of failures. It is a very curious thing to note that the stammerer is generally a fairly good subject. Moreover he will usually talk without any difficulty in the hypnotic trance. This is so much a relief to the sufferer that the writer has had cases in which the stammerer refused to wake up, pleading to remain hypnotized just a little longer so that he could really enjoy talking.

It is very difficult for the average reader to realize how very strong this power of popular prejudice may be. The writer has a friend, one of the great psychiatrists of the country, a former president of the American Psychiatric Association. This man made the statement that even if he were convinced of the value of hypnotism in treating nervous disorders he would not dare use it in his institution, one of the country's best state hospitals for nervous diseases. There would be too many unpleasant questions to be answered!

Yet this particular doctor is well known for courage and for broad-mindedness.

There is not one member of the medical profession in either Utica or Syracuse, to mention specific cities, who uses hypnotism in his practice. Why? Popular prejudice, nothing more The medical profession is the most liberal of all groups, but even medicine must bow to the popular will on certain subjects. This, unfortunately, is one. Yet the reader of this book will by now realize how much this is pure prejudice, how very little he knows of the real science of hypnotism. The stage hypnotist, the "professional," has so disgusted the average citizen with his exhibitions that it will be many years before hypnotism will regain the prestige which it now enjoys in Europe, where such stage shows are illegal.

Hypnotism has another possible use which will probably be

more carefully investigated as time passes. In many conditions rest and quiet are very necessary if a cure is to be effected. We cite tuberculosis as one example. It would seem that hypnotism is admirably suited to obtain this rest and relaxation. By this means the patient could be kept in trance during the "rest period" and, with the aid of suggestion, be convinced that his co-operation at all times was necessary to a cure.

More important, however, might be its use in certain treatments during which the patient suffers great discomfort, either at the time of treatment or afterward. The "fever cure" of various diseases, such as arthritis, gives us one such example. Here the patient undergoes the greatest discomfort and even becomes delirious as a result of the high fever induced by the treatment. If this individual were hypnotized in advance, he could be thrown into trance during the treatment and thus could be saved great suffering. In such a case hypnotism would be definitely superior to any drug, since we would not have to worry about possible complications.

Then again hypnotism might be of real use in one phase of curing the drug addict. Many patients refuse to take the cure because of the severity of those "withdrawal" symptoms. We mentioned before that these cause the most acute suffering on the part of the victim in question. If this patient could be put in trance we would at least overcome one barrier to the effective treatment of drug addiction.

Certain situations would lend themselves very nicely to a novel form of technique; namely, the use of the phonograph record. These can now be so conveniently prepared that they are no longer a novelty and it is quite possible for the operator to dictate his suggestions to the disc. Needless to say, these suggestions can vary for every specific case. The record will put the individual to sleep, give the necessary treatment in the doctor's own voice and then awaken the patient. There is nothing impossible, or to the psychologist, unusual in this attack. Such records are well known in his laboratory.

The writer is strongly of the opinion that this technique offers very great possibilities. One great objection to the use of hypnotism hinges on a question of time. The doctor must be in personal attendance and our treatment may well consume an hour. This is quite impractical in normal medical procedure. Doctors are very busy people. But with the victrola record he could prepare the record, after first preparing the subject and then give genuine "absent treatment." Such a device lends itself to the quack and the charlatan, but this is no reason why it cannot be used for quite legitimate medical ends.

At this point it seems right to give brief consideration to possible dangers which may accompany the use of hypnotism, especially in unskilled hands and when used for medical ends. First, and it seems to us, most obvious is the danger of treating "symptoms" rather than diseases. This is very well illustrated in the case of pain. There can be no doubt that hypnotism can relieve pain, but very grave doubt that it can relieve the cause of this pain, especially if it should be an organic cause.

The writer is quite certain that he could in many cases remove all pain accompanying an acute attack of appendicitis, but that would by no means cure the appendix. Quite the opposite By removing this danger signal he might very easily be responsible for a case of ruptured appendix, which might be fatal. Similarly a toothache may seem a very trivial affair, but the cure for toothache is a dentist, not a hypnotist. Pain is nature's great danger signal and we do not remove the danger of a crash simply by turning off the red light.

This has always been a potent criticism against the use of hypnotism as practiced by the old masters. It lent itself so very easily to the treatment of symptoms. Alcoholism could be cured in almost miraculous fashion, but it did not always occur to these folks that alcoholism was merely one symptom of a weak personality. Remove liquor and the craving for a retreat was still there. Similarly with many of the hysterical symptoms. Take away one of these "escapes" and the individual would come back one month later proudly flaunting another; and very frequently it was a worse symptom.

We must admit a certain truth in these criticisms. But now we can use hypnotism not only to cure the symptom but also to clear up the underlying difficulty, provided of course this is not organic. And hypnotism may be of considerable help in treating some organic complaints, more from the angle of obtaining proper co-operation from the patient. We are quite certain that some organic diseases as gastric ulcer, exophthalmic goiter, perhaps diabetes and even heart disease have a mental origin. They result from the strain of our high strung civilization on body organs which were not evolved for such an existence. While it seems very doubtful that we can reverse the process, that we can cure gastric ulcer by mental means, we can use hypnotism to aid in the treatment.

The hypnotist must guard against the subject becoming so very susceptible to the trance that he can be hypnotized by anyone, but this is a simple matter handled by suggestion while in hypnotism. Incidentally, as we mentioned in an earlier chapter, the operator need never worry about "awakening" his subject. He will rapidly find that the real problem is to induce sleep, not dispel it. Possible criminal uses of hypnotism we discuss in a later chapter. Blackmail, by the way, is always a danger. We have had some cases in which patients have even taken the matter to court, suing for enormous damages under the advice of some enterprising lawyer. This is a very real danger, and the answer is insurance with any reputable firm. The enthusiasm of this blackmailing type cools in remarkable fashion when they find they are to do business with the lawyers of a great insurance company. This form of protection can be written cheaply, since it generally guards against pure blackmail and as such will never call for court action.

The writer feels that the real danger in hypnotism lies to the operator himself, at least to the experienced operator. Never has he as yet seen a case wherein the subject has experienced any bad effects from hypnotism when this is used by a careful experienced hypnotist. So great, however, is popular prejudice in this field that this same operator may easily find himself in very hot water when this prejudice takes specific form and centers itself on one individual. For this reason the President of Colgate University forbade its use on the campus. This is certainly not due to any unreasoned reaction on his part for President Cutten was acknowledged the leading American authority on the subject in the early twentieth century.

Colleges are made that way. If the parent finds that his son is being used for such research purposes, his reactions may be very hostile. If he chooses to bring this matter to the attention of the board of trustees things may become very unpleasant indeed for the professor in question. The only safe answer to this situation is to use hypnotism with students only in specific cases where the consent of the parents has been obtained. This is frequently possible, especially when the student in question is low in his school work and the operator is able to offer some definite hope that, with the use of hypnotism he may be able to remedy matters in this field.

The same type of prejudice applies to the doctor. Any medical man who would dare use hypnotism in his daily practice might very easily commit professional suicide. Nor is there any remedy in sight at the present time. We must educate the layman to the point where he does not get a cold chill every time the subject is mentioned and have visions of a twentieth century dracula forcing his unhappy victims into horrible crimes against man and God. As the situation now stands there is far more danger to the hypnotist than the hypnotized.

The reader will note that we have given very little attention to the use of hypnotism in the diseases of everyday life. We have made this oversight intentionally because these conditions have been covered very fully by several of the older writers, as for example, Bernheim. We quote several cases from his work, *Suggestive Therapeutics,* as translated from the second French edition by Herter. We choose a random selection to illustrate the very wide use made of hypnotism by these older authorities.

For example, Observation 10[1] in his book is a case of chronic lead poisoning and final complete cure with the aid of hypnotism! Hardly a condition in which one would expect a "mental" cure.

Observation 20[2] is headed "Violent hysterical paroxysms dating back one year. Complete cure from time of first suggestion." This is more the type of ailment we would expect to find referred to hypnotism.

Observation 30[3]: "Nervous aphonia (loss of speech) of one month's standing. Cure by simple affirmation." All these cases have a description of the treatment following the case description.

Observation 40[4]: "Melancholy, insomnia, anorexia (loss of appetite). Rapid cure by hypnotic suggestion." Again more or less the sort of case on which we would expect to use hypnotism.

Observation 50[5]: "Trouble in writing consecutive to chorea. Cure in a single séance of hypnotic suggestion." The inability to write here was very marked and the cure clear-cut.

Observation 59[6]: "Nocturnal incontinence of urine since infancy, relieved by a single suggestion." Hypnotism is of definite use here.

Observation 71[7]: "Tubercular diathesis. Restoration of sleep and disappearance of thoracic pains by suggestion." Decidedly not what we would expect. Tuberculosis is not a "mental" condition by any stretch of the imagination.

Observation 80[8]: "Rheumatic paralysis of the forearm and right hand. Sensation totally restored in one séance. Total cure

---

[1] Bernheim, H., *Suggestive Therapeutics*, p. 257.
[2] Bernheim, H., *Suggestive Therapeutics*, p. 284.
[3] Bernheim, H., *Suggestive Therapeutics*, p. 302.
[4] *Ibid.*, p. 314.
[5] *Ibid.*, p. 330.
[6] *Ibid.*, p. 351.
[7] *Ibid.*, p. 364.
[8] *Ibid.*, p. 370.

in four séances." It sounds impossible but Bernheim was a very careful observer.

Observation 90[9] : "Lumbo-crural muscular pain with obstinate sacro-sciatic neuralgia dating back six months. Notable improvement after several hypnotic séances; almost complete cure after five weeks of repeated suggestion."

Observation 100[10] : "Sciatic pain dating back three days, cured by a single suggestion."

The reader will note that we quote every tenth case from Bernheim, departing from this order only when the cases are too technical for the reader to grasp. This gives us a very good idea of the diversity of the diseases, organic and non-organic which Bernheim treated. We would point out that Bernheim held an important position as professor in the faculty of medicine at Nancy, France. Should the reader care to check, he will find that Moll, Bramwell, Tuckey, and others report essentially the same type of result as does Bernheim. These also are respected names in the history of medicine. We do not discuss this application of hypnotism to the general practice of medicine because others much better qualified have already recorded the results where all the world may read.

There can be no doubt that hypnotism may be of great aid in curing many types of human disease. At the present moment, however, it has practically no real value in America. This is due entirely to popular prejudice, that curious quirk in human thinking which sees in hypnotism something closely allied to black magic and the supernatural. We must not blame the medical profession if our own ignorance and superstition robs them of this very valuable device for combatting human ailments. First, we must educate ourselves. We will then find that the doctor is the most easily educated of all humanity.

---

9 *Ibid.*, p. 382.
10 *Ibid.*, p. 393.

Chapter VII

HYPNOTISM IN CRIME

THERE are two aspects to this problem of hypnotism in crime. First, can it be used to further the commission of a crime and, secondly, can hypnotism be of use in the detection of criminal acts. Both are fascinating problems and both are still very much in the realm of speculation. We simply do not know, for in order to determine if the subject will commit a crime we must literally have him do so. No fake setup will satisfy our critics, although many of these experimental situations do come pretty close to giving us the real picture of a criminal act. But the hypnotic subject is so shrewd, so capable of detecting what is fake and what is reality that we cannot be sure unless the crime is genuine; and this would certainly never be reported in the literature.

Then we dare not use hypnotism in the detection of crime. So great is the prejudice against its use that any counsel for the defense could literally shatter the state's case if he could prove to the jury that the police had even attempted to use hypnotism. This is no blind assertion. It has already occurred.

Let us take a general survey of the situation with regard to this matter of crime in or as the result of hypnotism. First of all the statement that the human will do nothing in hypnotism which he will not do in the waking state. Utterly unproven and unquestionably false. We need but to watch the performance of a good stage hypnotist to realize that our friends would not make unqualified fools of themselves on the stage if they were in a "normal" condition. Hypnotism is first cousin to somnambulism. to talking in one's sleep, and we have cases in the literature where sleep talkers have literally "talked." Again we

165

have many cases of compulsions in ordinary life, such as the compulsion to steal or to set fires. We know that these are irresistible, we know further that they are in reality posthypnotic suggestions of a somewhat unusual type. We can infer that what we obtain here we could also obtain in hypnotism.

Why not make crucial experiments with hypnotism itself and find out? Because such experiments at once leave the experimenter open to criminal action and could never be reported in the literature. Will the subject steal one hundred dollars from his brother's pocket? Suppose we try. He either does or he does not which seems to depend on the operator and on operator attitude. With Erickson he does not, with Wells he does. But we get nowhere in either case. If he refuses the writer of this book will say it is a matter of attitude on the part of the operator. Erickson, one of the very best in the country, will naturally deny this but he will have a difficult time proving the contrary.

And if the experiment succeeds? Still unsatisfactory. The critic will say that the subject realized all along it was a hoax and only did the act to please the operator. To be sure, it looks genuine but what will happen if we pull this subject up before a judge, with the prospect of six months in jail staring him in the face. Will he still protect the hypnotist? No one knows for it cannot be tried. We cannot bring such things to court action for the court does not play. If that money was stolen, some one goes to jail, either subject or hypnotist, and no operator would dare take the risk. It would mean professional ruin in either case if he ever published his results.

The best we can do is to arrive at a conclusion of probably yes or probably no. The subject in hypnotism is not "asleep" in any sense of the word. He is just as wide awake as he ever was, just as alert, just as discerning. But he is highly suggestible and very co-operative. He will do anything to oblige the hypnotist, within certain limits.

But it is very important to note that those limits are very different with different people. Some people may refuse point blank to forge a check under any circumstances when in the trance, others appear to have no particular objection on the subject. The reader must bear in mind that we do not claim *all* good hypnotic subjects would commit a criminal act as the result of hypnotism. Far from it. We only assert that, from the evidence we have, it seems highly probable that many subjects would so do if urged on by a good operator.

Let us take one of the very best experiments as demonstrating the difficulty of proof. L. W. Rowland of Baylor University arranged a very ingenious apparatus to see if the hypnotized subject would act in such a way as to harm himself or others. He placed a rattlesnake in an open case and irritated the beast until it was in a very dangerous mood. Then he ordered his subjects to reach for the piece of rubber pipe. This sounds very dangerous but between the subject and the angry snake was a sheet of "invisible glass," a new preparation which is literally invisible, for it is so made that it reflects no light at all. Strangely enough, the subjects promptly reached for the snake and were saved only by this obstruction. The writer would have sworn that such an experiment would fail, which merely goes to show that one cannot tell beforehand what will happen.

Rowland now altered his procedure. He himself was to be the victim, so an assistant took over the handling of the subject while Rowland sat behind the invisible glass. The assistant explained to the subject just how dangerous sulphuric acid is, especially when it comes in contact with human flesh. Next he handed the subject a glass of genuine acid and suddenly said, "Throw it in his face." The subject promptly did so, Rowland being saved only by that invisible barrier.

Conclusive and satisfactory? Not at all, but the best work yet done along this particular line. Not conclusive because the critic can find at least one flaw in the experiment, possibly others. The writer took this report, on its publication, to one of our best authorities on hypnotism. He read it through and said at once, "How do you know that glass is invisible? To you, yes. But the hypnotic subject may, probably does, have much greater keenness of vision than does the normal individual."

He then referred to the type of experiment, mentioned in an earlier chapter, wherein the subject picked out his "mother's" picture—from an earlier hallucination—from twenty perfectly plain white calling cards by recognizing some trifling flaw in the surface of the card. Such skepticism is pretty hard to meet. Asked how it would be possible to have this experiment made "air tight" he replied, "Take away the glass."

"In that case there might be a corpse in the laboratory."

"Exactly. But I see no other way to meet the objection."

In other words, these experiments by Rowland would seem to indicate that *in all probability* a person will act in such a way as to injure himself or others as a result of hypnotic suggestion. To prove this to the satisfaction of science, he would literally need a corpse in the laboratory.

W. R. Wells at Syracuse University has also experimented along original lines in his investigation of the possible use of hypnotism for criminal ends. He uses what appears to the author as a much more promising line of attack in that he tries to avoid too great a conflict on the subject's part. His experiments have consisted mostly in having his subjects steal small sums of money from various acquaintances. He eases the shock by, for example, telling the subject that he himself left a dollar bill in the friend's room, thus producing a delusion that the money is really his own. Then the subject is instructed to get the same—and does so! Moreover Wells finds it very easy to remove all knowledge from these subjects of ever having been hypnotized.

This line of attack used by Wells seems to the writer excellent. He does everything possible to avoid conflict, to obtain the co-operation of his subjects, to "fool" them if you will by assisting the operator in an important psychological experiment. This line of approach seems to offer greater possibilities than the amazing "frontal" attack by Rowland. Every time the writer has tried Rowland's technique he has failed miserably, which does not in any way cast reflection on that investigator's work. The writer did not believe it possible and that old problem of operator-attitude came in. The subject realized this and behaved accordingly. On the other hand, the writer has succeeded in having a wealth of bogus checks forged by subjects who were merely co-operating in a psychological experiment. Needless to say, the checks in question were torn up before they caused any embarrassment.

Against this work of Wells, we can lodge that same type of objection which always meets us like a stonewall. What guarantee have we that the subject was not playing his usual farce, that he had picked up from other students that he was supposed to stage his "act" and that nothing serious would happen? No matter how carefully those Syracuse experiments are conducted, the critic can always fall back on this line of defense.

And what guarantee have we that the subject, if brought to trial, would not recall the whole thing and expose the operator? After all, if the crime were really serious and the subject were faced with ten years in prison or even death, the unconscious would have every reason in the world to "talk." The objection here seems almost unanswerable. A genuine trial and a genuine prison sentence would be about the only way to determine whether or not, in football parlance, the line would hold. There are ways around this danger, as we will later see, but those means could only be used in the genuine commission of crime.

M. H. Erickson at Eloise State Hospital, in sharp contrast with Wells, Rowland, and the author, finds no evidence whatsoever that the subject will commit criminal acts. Moreover, Erickson has probably had more experience with hypnotism than any of the others. He works in a setting where popular prejudice means nothing and he works hard. He finds that the subject balks at every suggestion of criminal action. But the writer feels this must be due to operator-attitude. The subjects realize Erickson expects negative results and they produce the same. The reader will note that the writer makes this statement quite out of "thin air," but he can see no other possible explanation. If one reliable group of investigators get positive results and if another finds the results wholly negative then we must seek some explanation. In this particular field of science the writer feels that operator-attitude is about the only way to explain the conflict, not only with reference to hypnotism and crime but elsewhere as in the case of Nicholson versus Young quoted in an earlier chapter.

We again stress the fact that hypnotism cannot be treated with the same outlook with which we approach the physical sciences. The speed of light is in no way dependent on the attitude of the experimenter, but the use of suggestion in any walk of life, including hypnotism, is so dependent. The orator is a success or a failure as he plays on our emotions and makes his suggestions with confidence and vigor. Suggestion works under the same laws, in hypnotism or out of the trance. It would seem just as difficult to predict the reaction of the hypnotic subject to a specific suggestion as it is to predict that of the individual member of a crowd listening to Hitler or Mussolini. "Probably" they will do so-and-so but then again they may not behave in such a way.

We would like also to insert a word on that very important factor of individual differences, so important to the whole field of psychology. The "average man" for example is a myth, a very useful abstraction for the statistician but he simply does not exist. We all differ one from the other, in size, or strength, intelligence or emotional control, "will power" or lack of the same. Similarly, even in the very best of subjects we would expect that we would find a very great range in their ability to resist criminal suggestions. If not, this is the only situation of the thousands with which psychology deals where there is absolute, even approximate, uniformity among all members of a large group. Such being the case we would reasonably suppose from our distribution according to the normal curve that we would find some subjects absolutely immune to any such suggestion from any operator. At the other extreme we could reasonably expect a group who would fall easy victims to almost any technique. In the middle, we would find the majority of subjects, people who would be reasonably resistant to a direct, frontal attack, so to speak, but who might be tricked into criminal action just as we can trick them into the trance by using the disguised technique.

Of course, we have no proof for this statement. It may be that the present war will give us the answer, for in war the belligerents are not worried over the ethics of a situation. They demand results. The use of hypnotism for either the commission or detection of crime is very similar to its possible uses in warfare, so we may find the answer to our question in this very unfortunate world situation, which we discuss in the following chapter.

But we would emphasize the fact that the question, as it now stands, is wide-open. We do not have the answer nor can we, from the very nature of the situation, hope to obtain this answer. Yet the question is of very serious importance, not only from the viewpoint of crime commission but, far more important, from that of crime detection. If hypnotism can be so used— and the writer is of the opinion that it can—then we may find it a very useful aid to our present methods of detecting crime.

Needless to say, the great barrier at present is that senseless prejudice which exists in the mind of the public. We must treat the criminal as a gentleman. As a nation we believe that everyone, including the murderer, should have a sporting chance. There is much to be said for this attitude—and much against it. To the writer it would seem that the criminal was no longer playing the game and could not demand that the rules apply in his case.

Let us consider some of the possible applications of hypnotism to criminal ends. Most of the actual work here has been done in Germany and we find it fairly well agreed that hypnotism could be used for sex offenses. Beyond this there is no such agreement.

There are several approaches to this problem. Would the criminal operator use the trance itself or would he prefer to work by means of the posthypnotic suggestion? Very probably the latter although there would be certain situations in which he could use the somnambulist himself without "waking" him up.

How would we expect him to proceed? If he were a criminal worthy of the name, then obviously not the way most of us have seen him presented in book and movie. There seems to be a tradition that, with hypnotism in crime we hypnotize our victim, hand him a club, and say, "Go murder Mr. Jones." If he refuses, then we have disproven the possibility of so using hypnotism. Such a procedure would be silly in the extreme. The skillful operator would do everything in his power to avoid an open clash with such moral scruples as his subject might have.

He would impress on the subject that he was taking part in some very important psychological experiments. Hypnotism gives a great increase in muscular control. Let us see how well he can forge Mr. Brown's signature.

After he has had practice in this and is reasonably good, we would go on to the next step. We are carrying on some interesting work with the police. We wish to convince them of the great importance of hypnotism. We are going to have him forge a few checks with Mr. Brown's signatures. We assure him they will be torn up at once and we will have a member of the police force handy to complete the picture. Would it work? The writer is almost certain that it would with certain subjects. The operator would be protected in that he would remove from his victim all knowledge of ever having been hypnotized and make it impossible for anyone else to hypnotize him at any future date.

Under such circumstances and using such a technique the

writer feels there is a very strong possibility that criminal acts could be obtained from a certain proportion of subjects, but the reader will see that it is impossible to tell just what would happen from then on. The subject forges a check, robs a home, or commits a murder in "good faith," if this is not too contradictory a use of terms. He is quite convinced that he is playing in another of those little farces which seem to give him so much pleasure. When this farce turns out to be very serious drama, when he finds himself facing a judge and jury with every prospect of disgrace and imprisonment, what then. Will he continue to protect the operator? No one knows for no one dares make the experiment.

In the eyes of the law he would still be guilty of forgery, robbery, or murder, but he might also indict the hypnotist. This might serve to ease his sentence but would not acquit him by any means. Drunkenness, for example, is no excuse for crime and neither is hypnotism. The reader will now see how very difficult it is to deal with certain of these questions. They are impossible of proof without the commission of actual crime, and that is beyond the province of the psychology laboratory.

But there are other possibilities of hypnotism in crime which have much greater chances of success. When we ask the individual bluntly to commit a murder, we are putting a tremendous strain on his moral code. We could only hope to succeed with the very best subjects. Should we try to trick him into a murder, we might succeed. The gun was loaded with dummy ammunition, he thought. Yet it is very open to question whether we could rely on his not exposing the hypnotist during the trial.

Suppose, however, we take a different line of attack. We use him to establish an alibi while we ourselves commit the crime. This might be just as effective from our point of view and would have a much better chance of success. Let us take a typical experiment. We hypnotize Smith in Oxford. He spends the afternoon and has tea with us, for our friend Brown has made some very cutting remarks on hypnotism and we decide he should be given a lesson. After the tea we retire to our room. Smith has been hypnotized all the time and Brown has never detected it.

"All right, Smith, wake up." Smith starts, looks puzzled, and is immediately "on guard." We find that many subjects adopt this attitude in such experiments. They realize in a vague sort of way that something has happened and are preparing to stall and "cover up" until they get the lay of the land.

We talk about sports for the next ten minutes. The subject does not recognize Brown although he has been in his company for the last three hours. Finally we came to the point.

"Where were you this afternoon?"

"In London. Spent the afternoon playing bridge with our friend, Black."

"You were in Oxford all afternoon and had tea with us here an hour ago," says Brown.

Smith has a sense of humor and is not caught off guard. He turns to the writer with a broad grin. "One of your friends from Amesbury? He looks all right to me but you never can tell." Amesbury is a State Hospital for Mental Diseases.

Brown is irritated. "Don't bluff. I say you were in Oxford all afternoon."

"Poor fellow! And he probably has a wife and children," is Smith's exasperating come-back as he retires into the afternoon paper. Needless to say, Smith, an excellent subject was acting under posthypnotic suggestion. He took an unholy delight in ragging Brown, for he had been told in trance that the latter believed hypnotism a hoax.

Brown was not to be put off. He told Smith he was lying and that the Black in London was a myth. Smith complacently agreed and suggested we drive him back to Amesbury. Finally, after much baiting of Brown he agreed to accompany us to London and see Black. The latter was also a fine subject and had been coached in advance.

Black met us at his apartment. "We've brought a friend to

see you," said Smith. "Not violent. Just a government guest at Amesbury. Come in, my Lord. This is the Duke of Normandy."

Brown stuck to his point. "Where was Smith this afternoon."

"Playing bridge in my apartment."

"He was having tea with me in Oxford."

"Oh, oh," said Black, "always best to humor them. You're quite right, Sir. He was undoubtedly having tea with you in Oxford. Do sit down."

"Where are the other two partners?"

"Sorry, Sir, but they just left by plane for Siberia. They have a pink fox farm there. Remarkable thing. Cross a purple martin with a Siberian Wumpus and you get a pink fox. Astonishing, don't you think? By the way, how is my good friend, Dr. Wright?" Wright is superintendent at Amesbury.

Poor Brown was literally stymied and took a terrible riding for the next quarter of an hour, but the worst was yet to come. He was getting more and more uncomfortable. Smith and Black obvious took him for a patient from Amesbury—as they had been instructed in hypnotism—and were delighted to have him at their mercy. Finally he arose.

"Well," he said testily, "I must be going."

"And where are you leaving for, Duke?"

"The station and Oxford."

"That's what you think," said Smith, "but actually you are going with us on a nice moonlight drive to your castle at Amesbury."

"Now, see here, this is going too far."

"Tut, tut, Duke. Think of the consternation at the regal residence if the Lord of the Manor turned up missing. We are your devoted slaves and you are going for a little ride. Come along." And along he went with the three of us.

Five miles outside Oxford we took mercy on him. He was asked to step into a "pub" for a moment. We followed not a minute later but all was now changed. The writer had removed the delusions when we sat down at his table. They did not even recognize Brown.

"Mr. Brown," he said, "I wish to introduce two friends, Smith and Black, both of Oxford. We are driving through. Why not come with us?"

From then on everyone was happy. Later in the evening Brown asked, "Where have you fellows been all day?"

"Oh, just driving around," said Black.

"You know," said Brown, "your friend here has a reputation as a hypnotist. Has he ever tried it on you fellows?"

"Between ourselves," said Smith, "that's what it is. A reputation. He couldn't hypnotize a cat. As for hypnotizing us, he's never been so foolish as to try. All pure bunk."

"Yes," said Brown, "That's what I thought a few hours ago."

"What's that?"

"Oh, nothing. Just thinking."

This silly episode really illustrates a great deal. Had the delusions not been removed Smith and Black would have insisted on their original story; namely that they had been playing cards in London all afternoon. Now, if we care to translate that into the field of crime, we see the ease with which we could prepare a watertight alibi. Needless to say, the subjects would have to be prepared well before hand and we could leave none of the loopholes which are so very evident in this silly experiment. But it could be done and would be a relatively simple trick. It would have three great advantages. First, the witnesses in question would believe absolutely in what they said. They would have nothing to cover up and, with careful preparation, their stories could be made to agree on all essentials.

Secondly, we would not have to depend for these alibis on shady figures from the criminal world. Any two or three good hypnotic subjects would be suitable, and these could and would be chosen from honorable and law abiding citizens.

Thirdly, there would be much less incentive for them to go back on their word and for the unconscious to expose the hypnotist. Not only are they in no personal danger themselves but they are telling what is to them a true story in the interest of a friend who is unjustly accused. That is a very different thing from being on trial themselves, faced with disgrace and imprisonment.

It is the writer's opinion that this line of attack would succeed with the majority of somnambulists. The reader must bear in mind, however, that this is pure conjecture. Such an experiment has never been tried, at least to the writer's knowledge. If tried, it certainly would never be reported in the literature. The difficulties encountered in arriving at any conclusive results in the field of hypnotism and crime are very great.

Then we have other possibilities, many in fact, but we will cite one more specific line of attack. We know that it is quite possible to induce hallucinations and delusions in hypnotism and that these can be made to carry over into the conscious state with great vividness. For example, the writer more by way of a joke than to prove a serious point, introduces a friend of his to two strangers. These latter are excellent hypnotic subjects and have been carefully coached as to their actions.

After a brief conversation the writer informs his friend that these two strangers have a very serious charge to make. Last night on Boar's Hill, just outside Oxford, they saw him run down and kill a pedestrian, then leave the scene without reporting to the police. The night was foggy—common enough around Oxford—and he evidently did not see their car parked in a lane not ten feet away. What did he propose to do about it?

Needless to say, the friend in question was flabbergasted. As a matter of fact, he had been on Boar's Hill the night previous and a man had been found dead by the side of the road, hit by a car. Moreover, this chap had a reputation for reckless driving. On a foggy night he might very easily have struck a man walking by the edge of the road and been none the wiser. The two strangers in question, both friends of the writer, had also been on the hill to a bridge party, so the situation could have been very nasty. As it was, however, the accused was quickly relieved by the assurance that the whole thing was a joke, but not before he realized that the two witnesses quite believed their story and intended to take action with the police.

May we add that it is best not to play tricks like this on your friends if you hope to keep them as friends. Even though the delusions were removed from the minds of the two witnesses and they behaved like gentlemen from then on, the shock was so great to the accused that he avoided the group in question in the future.

The reader will see the ease with which an unscrupulous operator could "frame" an innocent man, and no one any the wiser. The witnesses would be telling a perfectly straight and true story. They saw it with their own eyes, so they believe it. They actually saw Jones enter the burglarized bank, push his wife into the river, or forge a check for five thousand dollars. To the witness there can be no doubt as to the truth of this statement, nor has he any great moral struggle to overcome if he sticks to his story. He is in no danger himself and he is helping the law in bringing a criminal to justice.

The reader will now begin to appreciate our impatience with those writers who make the blanket statement that it is impossible to induce criminal actions in the hypnotic subject. Erickson alone has actually experimented on the subject to any great extent and his opinion certainly carries weight. None more so and the writer of this book may yet have to eat his words that Erickson's negative results are due to operator attitude. But we must make that statement at the present moment, and await further results.

But other writers who adopt this negative viewpoint use so terribly little imagination. Apparently there is only one way to have a subject commit a crime. We hypnotize him for the first time at 10:00 A.M. At 10:30 we hand him a knife and say, "Go murder your father." The old gentleman is still hale and hearty by 11:00 A.M. so we have proved our point. If the gentleman in question had been murdered, the writer, for one, would have been very much astonished. Things just don't happen that way.

When we discuss the possibility of using hypnotism for criminal ends we must credit the hypnotist in question with being intelligent and with having imagination. He will do everything in his power to avoid any too direct collision with this victim's moral sense. He will also recognize that subjects in somnambulism are almost as different as are normal people. To be sure all are suggestible to an unusual degree but when these suggestions cross their ethical standards, then every law of distribution would tell us that some can resist such suggestions with much greater effectiveness than can others.

In sober reality there would seem to the writer very little danger from hypnotism in crime. Granted a highly skilled and intelligent operator, the possibilities might be great. But there are very few such people in this country and none of them have as yet established a criminal record. Any "amateur" or unskilled enthusiast would be almost certain to bungle the job. He would not realize the limitations of hypnotism, the fact that people in hypnotism are very different, the necessity of not antagonizing the individual's ethical standards. He would be pretty certain to end in jail.

We must bear in mind that hypnotism, pretty much in its present form, has been known since the days of Liebeault in the 1860's. Yet in eighty years' time we have few if any authentic cases of its use for criminal ends. This does not prove too much but it does prove that its use for such purposes is neither easy nor obvious. The criminal would quickly have absorbed it in his technique had the case been otherwise. Our modern improvements in methods and the active investigation of this subject have reawakened a very grave possibility of the use of hypnotism for criminal ends but even so it would never be a tool for the incompetent amateur. He has tried it too often already and has always come to grief.

The police are fully aware of any dangers which may be inherent in hypnotism and would be quite competent to uncover the work on any but the most skillful operator. Even in his case we are still faced with the unsolved problems we have outlined in previous pages. No one knows the answer for the question is unanswerable without the actual commission of a criminal act. We can assure the reader, for his own peace of mind, that our Federal Bureau of Investigation, for example, is fully aware of every possibility in connection with hypnotism and is extremely efficient in all its activities.

Let us now turn to the other side of this fascinating picture. Hypnotism might be used for criminal ends within the limits we have already outlined. Can we reverse the process? Can we use hypnotism in the detection of crime? It certainly has its possibilities. Up to the present popular prejudice has prevented any police department from openly using this device, but we can look forward to a time when this prejudice may not be quite as unreasonable.

From the viewpoint of logic the human is totally irrational. He will permit our police to use "third degree" methods which may be pretty brutal but hypnotism? Never! Of course, we, as individuals, disapprove of the third degree, but, on the other hand, we don't get "all het up" about it. That is a matter for the police to handle and we more or less let them suit themselves. But those same police know very well that if any police department dared to openly use hypnotism in the detection of crime, the public might get very much "het up" over such a thing. Yet hypnotism would be far less brutal than the mildest third degree. And it might be much more effective. Truly the human mind does work in fearful and wonderful ways.

Perhaps the most evident use we could make of hypnotism in the detection of crime would be that of obtaining information. We at once are confronted with the same old question, will the subject talk. There is very little evidence either for or against, but in the opinion of the writer there will be a certain proportion at least of suspected or convicted criminals who, under direct questioning, will talk.

But why use direct questioning. Why try to use a club when there is much better chance of success with more subtle tactics. The police are seeking information and are not particular how it is obtained so long as it throws light on the case. The hypnotic subject has a memory which is often startlingly good for past events. So we play a little game with him in hypnosis which apparently has nothing to do with the crime in question. We are interested, we tell him, in having him demonstrate to us how well he can recall events in the past. Where, for instance, was he on Christmas Day a year ago and what was he doing? Then where was he two years ago? And three years? Then how about July Fourth in the same order?

All this questioning is done by the prison doctor or some one quite unconnected with the authorities. Moreover, the specific crime with which he is charged is never mentioned. But the police knew very well that there is always hope if the accused will talk on any subject. There is a very good chance that he will let fall the clues which, when bound together, will lead to his confederates, his "hideouts," and finally to his conviction. Only after we had tried this method described above would we resort to direct questioning. All this would, of course, be with a subject who had been hypnotized by the disguised method, who knew nothing of ever having been hypnotized and could be hypnotized by no one else.

What is the objection to using hypnotism on the criminal in this fashion? Popular prejudice, which is so strong that no law enforcement body has, as yet, had the courage to try, except in one or two very isolated instances. So strong is the feeling of the public on this matter that any lawyer or district attorney knows quite well that his case would be "shot" if the other side could prove he had attempted the use of hypnotism.

As a matter of fact, proof is quite unnecessary. The writer knows of one case wherein the prosecuting attorney was also known to be interested in hypnotism. The case for the defense looked almost hopeless when the lawyer for the defense had a brilliant idea. He coached the prisoner to claim that the state's attorney had attempted to hypnotize him before the trial. From then on the jury was definitely sympathetic toward the prisoner and the state lost the case.

Perhaps one of the most interesting possibilities for the use of hypnotism in crime is that of building up an informer service along the lines we later suggest for hypnotism and counter-espionage in warfare. By the use of the disguised technique we locate a number of good hypnotic subjects among the criminal class. We then isolate and train these subjects, coaching them in hypnotism to look for certain information which is very much needed by the forces of law and order.

Under such posthypnotic suggestions, as explained in the next chapter, the subject would keep his "unconscious ear" always cocked in the direction of such information, but consciously he would have no knowledge of what he was doing. He would be promised immunity and reward in hypnotism for his acts, so as to insure his loyalty. Then every so often the police net would gather him in on some minor charge, collect the information and release the prisoner in question. Such a suggestion will impress the reader as being quite impossible but we suggest he read through the next chapter before passing any hasty judgment. There is nothing at all impossible about such a procedure.

This line of attack would have a great advantage. The informer would have no conscious knowledge of his activities and this conviction of innocence would be his greatest protection. Moreover consciously he would know nothing so that any attempt at forcing him to betray the scheme would be of little use. Lastly, we would not have any very strong ethical code to combat in this group of people. Given the proper incentive many of them would be far more willing to betray their friends than would the average reader of this book.

Such a technique has other interesting possibilities. Given a free hand, the authorities could proceed to plant such prepared subjects from the criminal class where it would do most good, in penitentiaries, prisons, and in criminal areas of our large cities, always with the idea of obtaining information which might, sooner or later, be of real use to the police.

There is another important fact which we must bear in mind about the use of hypnotism. Criminals, as a class, are not overly intelligent. They have a healthy fear of anything they do not understand. This we see clearly in the use of the so-called lie-detector, a very impressive piece of psychological apparatus which by the measurement of blood pressure, rate and depth of breathing, and the psycho-galvanic reflex is often able to detect the fact that the accused is lying. To this apparatus we now add the ophthalmograph, a neat instrument which photographs the subject's eye movements. These seem to behave differently under emotional strain, as when the subject is trying to "cover up" a crime.

A friend in a police department tells a humorous story which illustrates just how the criminal can often be bluffed into a confession. Pete was accused of embezzlement amounting to over one hundred thousand dollars. The case hinged around forgery. Several specimens of the forged signature had been found in Pete's room, but Pete resolutely denied all knowledge of these. If it could be proved that he had practiced these signatures it would be easy to convict, but Pete was an old hand at this game. Try as they would the authorities could not trap him into a confession. It was finally decided to use the lie-detector in a last effort to get a statement.

The lie-detector as we mentioned before is a very impressive piece of apparatus. All sorts of electrical attachments with three pens writing automatically on a moving strip of paper. Pete was introduced to the monster and was obviously uneasy. Then it was explained to him that this lie-detector was sure to catch him if he told a lie and he was "hooked up." The investigator asked several noncommital questions and then said:

"Pete, do you know who forged those signatures we found in your room?"

"I do," said Pete, to the amazement of the police.

One or two more irrelevant questions and then.

"Pete, did you forge those signatures yourself?"

"I did," said Pete.

That tied up the case but, as the official humorously said, the lie-detector was a flat failure. There was no lie to detect. But it did frighten the culprit into a confession. One of the main uses of hypnotism might be right along these lines. It would be held as an unknown, mysterious threat over the head of the accused, and in many cases the accused might be so impressed that he would convict himself, as did Pete.

The reader cannot fail to be impressed with the very unsatisfactory nature of things in so far as the use of hypnotism in the detection of crime is concerned. But if he is quite fair he will also realize that this is no fault of science. The research worker is willing, even anxious, to help law enforcement along these lines, but he is also anxious to stay out of the penitentiary. As things now stand, popular prejudice is so strong that he might very easily find himself in serious trouble if he became a little over-enthusiastic in his investigations.

Chapter VIII

HYPNOTISM IN WARFARE

FOR some unknown reason the general public places hypnotism in the same class as black magic, voodooism and spiritism. Even when he sees a genuine demonstration on the stage or in the laboratory the layman is still unconvinced. The subject was either bluffing or, in the case of the stage demonstration, results were produced by magic "à la Houdini." First let us make one point quite clear. The psychologist is the only person entitled to an opinion on this subject, just as the chemist alone can pronounce on a chemical formula or the astronomer give a valid opinion on the movement and weight of the planets.

No competent psychologist in this country would dare write an article denying the existence of hypnotism, the fact that certain phenomena such as "visions," paralysis, analgesia (insensitivity to pain) and total loss of memory for occurrences in the "trance," can be produced in his laboratory. So we are not interested in proving to the reader that hypnotism exists.

Our interest here lies in some of the more unfamiliar sides of hypnotism which may make it of use in warfare. Again, no psychologist would deny the existence of such phenomena. But some would very emphatically deny our proposal that these states and conditions could be used for the ends which we suggest. The reason for this skepticism is obvious, if we but consider the situation. Hypnotism in crime, either for the commission or solution of criminal acts is very closely related to the possible use of hypnotism in warfare.

The only possible way of determining whether or not a subject will commit a murder in hypnotism is literally to have

185

him commit one. No "fake" setup will satisfy the critics, for the hypnotised subject is not "asleep." He is very wide awake, willing to co-operate in all kinds of fake murders with rubber knives. But with a real knife or a loaded revolver? No one knows, for the simple reason that no one dares find out. The police would not see the point when they viewed the corpse and were told it was the result of a "scientific" experiment. Nor would the jury. Sing Sing and the electric chair would probably put an end to the career of the particular "scientist."

But warfare may, undoubtedly will, answer many of these questions. A nation fighting with its back to the wall is not very worried over the niceties of ethics. If hypnotism can be used to advantage we may rest assured that it will be so employed. Any "accidents" which may occur during the experiments will simply be charged to profit and loss, a very trifling portion of that enormous wastage in human life which is part and parcel of war.

Let us glance at certain aspects of hypnotism with which the general reader may not be familiar. He probably is familiar with the general picture of the hypnotic trance, whether this be produced in the quiet of the laboratory or the glare of the stage. He knows that people can be thrown into this trance and while in it will do weird things. On the stage they will, at the suggestion of the operator, hunt elephants with a broomstick or fish for whales in a goldfish bowl. They will prance around the stage on all fours, barking like a dog or give a good imitation of Lincoln in his *Gettysburg Address*. They will strip off most of their clothes at the command of the hypnotist or stiffen out between two chairs while he breaks rocks on their chest.

The reader knows of this. To be sure he may suspect that it is all "bunk," but he at least realizes what is supposed to take place. Suffice it to say here that it *does* take place and *can* be quite genuine. The psychologist in his laboratory may not favor quite so flashy performance, but he can duplicate the tricks of the best stage "professional."

There are other sides to hypnotism far more important than

those shown on the stage for the benefit of a wondering audience. One in every five adult humans can be thrown into the hypnotic trance—somnambulism—for which they will have no memory whatsoever when they awaken. From the military viewpoint there are a few facts which are of great interest. Can this prospective subject,—this "one-in-five" individual—be hypnotized against his will? Very obviously no prisoner of war will be co-operative if he knows that the hypnotist is looking for military information. Nor will any ordinary citizen if he suspects that the operator will use him to blow up a munitions plant.

The answer to this first very vital question is "yes." We do not need the subject's consent when we wish to hypnotize him, for we use a "disguised" technique. The standard way to produce hypnotism in the laboratory is with the so-called sleep technique. The operator "talks sleep" to the subject, who eventually relaxes and goes into a trance, talking in his sleep and answering questions just as will many people of our acquaintance in everyday life. Now suppose we set up a neat little psychological experiment on relaxation. That sounds harmless enough. We attach a blood pressure gauge to the subject's right arm and the psycho-galvanic reflex to the palm of his hand, just to make everything look "shipshape." These devices are for measuring his ability to relax, just impressive little gadgets to remove any suspicion.

Next we tell the subject he is to imagine himself falling sound asleep, since this will aid in his attempts to relax. We also point out that, of course, the very highest state of relaxation will be his ability actually to fall into a deep sleep while we are talking to him. Needless to say we also stress the great importance of the ability to relax in this modern world of rush and worry, promising to show him how to get results as one end of these experiments. All this by way of "build up." Probably not one of the readers of this chapter would realize that this was preparation for hypnotism, but would co-operate willingly in this very interesting psychological experiment.

We then proceed to "talk sleep," much the same as in ordinary hypnosis, carefully avoiding any reference to a trance or making any tests with which the subject might be familiar, all the while checking on blood pressure and psycho-galvanic reflex to keep up the "front." Finally we make the test of somnambulism or deep hypnotism. We see if the subject will talk to us in his sleep without awakening. If this does not succeed, the subject wakes up completely, and in this case we simply repeat the experiment hoping for better luck next time. But if we do succeed, if the individual belongs to the "one-in-five" club, the subject is just as truly hypnotized as by any other method, and from now on everything is plain sailing. By use of the post-hypnotic suggestion we assure ourselves there will no be trouble the next time. We simply say, "Listen carefully. After you wake up I will tap three times on the table with my pencil. You will then have an irresistible impulse to go sound asleep." The next trance is just that easy to get, and the subject has no idea that it is the pencil which has put him off.

Let us follow this process a little farther. The operator has succeeded in hypnotising the subject without his consent if not against his will. It is the same thing so far as practical results are concerned. But in this war situation he must go further if he is to attain the results for which he is striving. There must be no leakage, no talking outside the classroom. So the operator now removes from the subject all knowledge that he has ever been hypnotized. This sounds weird to the reader but is quite simple, again by the use of suggestion in the trance. We tell the subject in hypnotism that on awakening he will have no remembrance of ever having been hypnotized, that if questioned he will insist he knows nothing about hypnotism and has never been a subject.

But we must go even farther than this. Once a person has become accustomed to hypnotism, has been repeatedly hypnotized, it becomes very easy for any operator to throw him into the trance. Obviously this will never do if we are to use hypnotism in warfare. So we plug this gap again by suggestion in the somnambulistic state. We assure the subject that in the future no one will be able to hypnotize him except with the special consent of the operator. This takes care of things very nicely.

The picture we now have is quite different from that which the reader has associated with hypnotism. We sit down with the subject in the laboratory. As we are talking on the latest boxing match the operator taps three times on the table with his pencil. Instantly—and we mean instantly—the subject's eyes close and he is sound "asleep." While in trance he sees a black dog come into the room, feels the dog, goes to the telephone and tells its owner to come get it. The dog is of course purely imaginary. We give him an electric shock which would be torture to a normal person, but he does not even notice it. We straighten him out between two chairs and sit on his chest while he recites poetry. Then we wake him up.

He immediately starts talking about that boxing match! A visitor to the laboratory interrupts him.

"What do you know of hypnotism?"

The subject looks surprised, "Why, nothing."

"When were you hypnotized last?"

"I have never been hypnotized."

"Do you realize that you were in a trance just ten minutes ago?"

"Don't be silly! No one has ever hypnotized me and no one ever can."

"Do you mind if I try?"

"Not at all. If you want to waste your time it's all right with me."

So the visitor, a good hypnotist, tries, but at every test the subject simply opens his eyes with a bored grin. Finally he gives up the attempt and everyone is seated as before. Then the original operator taps on the table with his pencil. Immediately the subject is in deep hypnotism.

Finally to complete this weird picture we can coach the

subject so that in the trance state he will behave exactly as in the waking state. Under these circumstances we could defy any reader, even a skilled psychologist, to tell whether the subject were "asleep" or "awake." To be sure there are tests which will tell the story but in warfare we cannot run around sticking pins into every one we meet just to see if he is normal.

So rapid can this shift be from normal to trance state, and so "normal" will the subject appear in trance that the writer has used such a subject as a bridge partner. He plays one hand in trance and one hand "awake" with no one any the wiser.

With this picture of hypnotism in mind let us see what we might do with it in actual war conditions. The reader is asked to note that from here we jump into the realm of theory. All these problems are still in the process of investigation, with (let us note) the Germans easily leading the field. Practically no articles have appeared on this use of hypnotism, but on a closely allied field, namely that of hypnotism in crime. The Germans, and they alone, have already done some excellent work here.

First and most obvious is that question of obtaining information from prisoners of war. Will the subject "talk" in hypnotism? We give the senatorial answer, "Yes, and then again no." Frankly, we are in ignorance on this point but the weight of evidence in the writer's opinion leans very definitely to "yes."

Let us see how we would proceed. The obvious line of attack is through the prisoners. There are always plenty of these in modern warfare, with a good percentage in hospitals. So we begin at the hospital as the logical point of contact. The operator, in the role of a doctor, chooses his battleground. Next he explains to the patients he has selected that he wishes to try on them the effect of relaxation. This sounds reasonable enough, especially in view of the fact that many of them would be in a highly agitated state, many would be "shell shock" cases. These, by the way, make excellent hypnotic subjects.

So the doctor proceeds to show these patients how to relax, which is merely the disguised technique of hypnotism we have already mentioned. In most cases he will not get the deep hypnotic trance of somnambulism, but neither will the patient realize the real end of the experiment. So no harm is done. But with at least one in five—probably more in these hospital cases—he will induce hypnotism. Then it is a simple matter to isolate this patient in a separate room and see what information can be obtained. First the hypnotist would remove from him all knowledge of ever having been hypnotized and make it impossible for anyone else to throw him into a trance without the operator's consent.

Now as to procedure. Someone has said there are two ways to kill a cat. One is to mess him all up with a club; the other is to persuade him that chloroform is good for fleas. The reader always seems to think that the next move would be to use "strong arm" methods, to apply the third degree. Not necessarily. We would need just as skillful questioning as that used by the F. B. I. and would have to try various devices on these prisoners—for we would not work with only one.

For example, we might call the prisoner before a group of enemy officers, our own men dressed as such and speaking his language. These would explain to him that they were very anxious to get information about conditions at the front and promise him promotion for his co-operation.

Or again, and probably more effective, we might work to undermine his morale. We would point out to him in hypnotism how badly he had been treated by his own army. A man of his abilities should obviously have a higher rank than he holds. And beside that, his government was not treating his family as it should. Now if he would just come over on our side of the war we would promise him promotion and recognition.

The reader is asked to remember that, in hypnotism the individual is highly suggestible. To be sure there is a popular belief that he will do nothing in the trance that he will not do in the working state. This is sheer nonsense. The writer has seen more than one stage performance wherein respected members of the community have made fools of themselves in public, an exhibition they would almost certainly never give if normal. On at least three occasions these subjects have later tried to "beat up" the hypnotist for his part in the affair. It is simply a question of degree. We also have cases in the records of hypnotism wherein subjects have given fraternity secrets or talked of very private love affairs.

A great deal also depends on operator attitude. If the subject suspects that the operator doubts his success or expects the experiment to be a failure, it will fail. But if the operator is himself convinced he will succeed, then he will succeed, at least in some cases. We must bear in mind that success is neither necessary nor to be expected every time. If the hypnotists isolated twelve good subjects in one day, and if only two of these would "talk" freely, his efforts would have been amply repaid. We do not for one moment claim that hypnotism is a "sure fire" method of getting information from prisoners of war. We simply claim that *with certain subjects* it will be highly successful. The weight of evidence points in this direction.

But this matter of receiving information from prisoners of war is only one of many possible uses of hypnotism in the war situation. There is also the possibility of spreading false information. This, to be sure would not be as useful as the first proposal but it would have its place in the military setup. For example, we take a subject and say to him. "Yesterday afternoon you were at Floyd Bennett Field. You saw there three anti-aircraft batteries. Here is a map of the field and here are the exact locations of these batteries. You will remember this very clearly after you wake up. Moreover, you will take the first opportunity to escape and give this news to your friends." Then we awaken him and make sure that he has every possible opportunity to escape. We even help him on his way.

This, of course, is only a trifling example for the purposes of illustration. But in actual warfare it might easily lead to disʻ aster. Suppose we hypnotize a captured officer of high rank. We show him a map of our front, pointing out to him that the weak point is between the cities of Utica and Syracuse. We have just withdrawn four divisions to reinforce the line further south. A heavy attack here may break the entire line. Then we take care he is allowed to escape with this information. If the trick worked it might easily turn the tide of a whole campaign.

Again we do not say it will work in all cases. Nothing so foolish. We do say that, in our opinion, it will work *with some subjects* and that such subjects can be picked out and trained very carefully before the crucial test is made. This idea that we hypnotize Colonel Smith today, then expect him to win the war for us tomorrow is folly. We might have to test, train and work with him for six months. Then he might be a very important aid in winning the said war. And we are not talking about *a* prisoner but hundreds of them.

May the writer point out that no one knows the answer to these proposals. No satisfactory experiments have yet been done on the subject. To be sure, M. H. Erickson has done excellent work, proving to his satisfaction that such uses of hypnotism would be quite impossible. But W. R. Wells and L. W. Rowland have done excellent work, proving just the opposite. So we may cancel them out with a strong scientific presumption that in certain cases at least it *is* possible. It would seem to the writer that this conflict in results is largely due to operator attitude, a fact, largely overlooked up to now, which has a strongly clouding effect on many experiments. *So if any brother psychologist should make the dogmatic statement that the uses we here propose for hypnotism are quite impossible, we are quite justified in saying that, as a scientist, he also is quite impossible.* We must admit that no one knows the answer, but we at least contend that the weight of evidence is in our favor. That leaves the subject wide-open.

Then we have a further possible use for hypnotism in warfare.

We are all aware, at least in a popular sense, of the difficulty of transmitting information. Codes are excellent, but we have highly trained men in our intelligence department who are also excellent in breaking down these codes. What man has done man can undo. If one expert can build up a code, another can break it down and find the meaning, given a few hours and adequate help. Then again a code must be printed somewhere and in warfare the enemy will pay good cash to get his hands on the printed page. Code books vanish no matter how carefully guarded, for the "international spy" of movie fame is a very real and a very clever person when the reward is big enough.

Of course we can always send documents by messenger. That also has its headaches. War is grim business, and life is cheap. If the enemy knows where these documents are, he will stop at nothing, neither robbery nor murder, in order to get the same. And human nature is weak. The nightmare of any intelligence service is a big, glowing double cross. Someone described an honest politician as one who would stay bought, and spies have a very bad reputation along these lines. We have already had some pretty ghastly examples of that in the recent war.

With hypnotism we can at least take care of one phase of our private messenger. We hypnotize our man in, say, Washington. In hypnotism we give him the message. That message, may we add, can be both long and intricate. A really intelligent individual can memorize a whole book if necessary. Then we start him out for Australia by plane with the instructions that no one can hypnotize him under any circumstances except Colonel Brown in Melbourne. By this device we overcome two difficulties. It is useless to intercept this messenger. He has no documents and no amount of "third degreeing" can extract the information, for the information is not in the conscious mind to extract. We could also make him insensitive to pain so that even the third degree would be useless.

Secondly, with this hypnotic messenger we need have no

worry about the double cross. In hypnotism we could build up his loyalty to the point where this would be unthinkable. Besides, he has nothing to tell. Consciously he has no idea of what he is doing. He is just a civilian with a business appointment in Australia, nothing more. He will give no information, for he has none to give. By this device we could make it much safer to send information when and where the private messenger could be used.

One of the most fascinating ideas with which to play in this use of hypnotism in warfare runs somewhat as follows. Let us take a laboratory experiment by way of background. For example, we can hypnotize a man in an hotel in, say, Rochester. We then explain to him in hypnotism that we wish the numbers and states of all out-of-state cars parked in the block surrounding the hotel. He is to note these very carefully in his unconscious mind but will have no conscious memory of having done so.

Then we awaken him and ask him, in the waking state to go out and get us a tube of toothpaste. He leaves the hotel and wanders around the block in search of that tube. Finally he returns, apologizing for his delay, saying that it was necessary for him to go entirely around the block before he noticed a drugstore in the very building itself. This, he says, was very stupid of him but apparently men are made that way. Did he notice anything of interest as he made his walk? "Nothing! Oh, yes, there was a dog fight down at the corner." And he described the battle in detail.

We now hypnotize him. He knows what we are seeking and at once proceeds to give us numbers and states of strange cars, very pleased with the fact that he can recall eighteen. He evidently enjoys the game immensely and is quite proud of his memory. Then we awaken him and see what he knows in the conscious state.

"How many cars are there around the building?"

"I don't know."

"How many out-of-state licenses are there around the building."

"Good heavens, I have no idea. I think there is a California car near the front entrance, but I have no idea as to its number."

A friend tries his hand.

"Now look here. You were hypnotized half an hour ago and you left this room under posthypnotic suggestion."

The subject gets irritated. "Look here yourself. I'm getting tired of that silly joke. This is the third time today you've pulled it. All right. I was hypnotized and saw pink elephants all over the lobby. Have it your own way." And the subject sits down to a magazine, obviously angry that this man cannot find something more amusing to say. It is interesting to note how often the hypnotic subject will react in this manner. Push him just a little too far and he becomes irritated. Obviously a very neat trick of the unconscious to end the argument and avoid any danger of being found out.

There are some very interesting possibilities to this experiment if we care to use it in warfare. For example, we take a very good hypnotic subject and send him to Cuba. We choose this country because such a situation would be absurd. He is an employee of the X Oil Company and as such his only conscious interest is to see that his organization is well run and does a profitable business.

But, in his unconscious mind he has other intentions. The aggressive Cubans are building a great naval base at Havana, an obvious menace to our overseas trade. So we station this man with his oil company in this city. Neither he nor the group in question need know anything of the arrangements. The instructions to his unconscious in hypnotism are very definite. Find out everything possible about the naval base. He is shown maps of this before he goes and coached as to just what is important. Nor is he ever allowed to submit written reports.

Everything must be handed on by word of mouth to one of the very few individuals who are able to hypnotize him.

Under these circumstances we may count on this man doing everything in his power to collect the information in question. The reader's very natural reaction is, "Why all this rigmarole. Why not have any keen executive of that oil company do the job without calling in the added trouble of hypnosis?"

There are certain safeguards if we use hypnotism. First, there is no danger of the agent selling out, but this would probably not be of great importance in this particular case. More important would be the conviction of innocence which the man himself had, and this is a great aid in many situations. He would never "act guilty" and if ever accused of seeking information would be quite honestly indignant. This conviction of innocence on the part of a criminal is perhaps his greatest safeguard under questioning by the authorities. Finally, it would be impossible to "third degree" him and so pick up the links of a chain. This is very important, for the most hardened culprit is always liable to "talk" if the questioners are but ruthless enough.

Far more useful than the foregoing purpose, however, would be that for a counterespionage service, built along the same lines. This would require both care and time to perfect, but once working it might prove extremely effective. Here the best approach would probably be through those of enemy alien stock within our own gates. Once again let us choose the aggressive Cubans as examples. In the event of war, but preferably well before the outbreak of war, we would start our organization. We could easily secure (say) one hundred or one thousand excellent subjects of Cuban stock who spoke their language fluently, and then work on these subjects.

In hypnotism we would build up their loyalty to this country; but out of hypnotism, in the "waking" or normal state we would do the opposite, striving to convince them that they had a genuine grievance against this country and encouraging them to engage in "fifth column" activities. Here we would be coming very close to establishing a case of "dual personality." There is nothing at all impossible in this. We know that dual, and even multiple, personality can be both caused and cured by hypnotism. Moreover, that condition, the Dr. Jekyll and Mr. Hyde combination, is a very real one once it is established.

They would, as we before said, be urged in the waking state to become fifth columnists to the United States, but we would also point out to them in hypnotism that this was really a pose, that their real loyalty lay with this country, offering them protection and reward for their activities. Through them we would hope to be kept informed of the activities of their "friends," this information, of course being obtained in the trance state. They would also be very useful to "plant" in concentration camps or in any other situation where it was suspected their services might be of real use to our intelligence department.

Once again these people would have a great advantage over ordinary "informers." Convinced of their own innocence, they would play the fifth column role with the utmost sincerity, and, as mentioned before, this conviction of innocence would probably be their greatest protection. Again, if suspected, no one could obtain from them any useful information. Only a very few key people could throw them into the trance and, without this, any attempts to get information would be useless. Finally, we again point out that we are fully aware of the difficulties which would be encountered in building up such an organization. Not one somnambulist in, say, ten, even one hundred, might be suitable for such work; and the determining of this suitability would be no easy task. But it *could* be done, and once accomplished would repay amply all the trouble.

A further extension of this same proposal would carry the war into the enemies' country, into Cuba in this case. These subjects would be admirable to "plant" in the enemies' own army with a view to obtaining information, or even for the ends of civilian sabotage.

And speaking of sabotage, this is probably one of the most dangerous fields, so far as the use of hypnotism in warfare is concerned. Here we see very clearly illustrated the folly of taking an arbitrary statement for granted, namely that the subject in hypnotism will do nothing against his moral nature. Just to clear up this point let us take a possible situation from the use of hypnotism for criminal ends. Will the subject commit murder in hypnotism? Highly doubtful—at least without long preparation, and then only in certain cases of very good subjects with, shall we say, no particular moral code.

Yet, strange to say, most good subjects will commit murder. In the writer's opinion there can be very little doubt on this score. They commit a legal, but not an ethical murder, so to speak. For example, we hypnotize a subject and tell him to murder you with a gun. We hand him a loaded revolver. In all probability he will refuse. Frankly for very obvious reasons, the writer has never made the experiment. Corpses are not needed in psychological laboratories.

But a hypnotist who really wished a murder could almost certainly get it with a different technique. Tomorrow, at three P.M., you will undoubtedly be in your office. So just before three he hypnotizes the subject, tells the subject to go at once to your office, point the gun at you and pull the trigger.

Then he remarks to his assistant that, of course, the gun is loaded with dummy ammunition, and that the operator is putting through a very important experiment for the police in order to prove the possible use of hypnotism in crime. He would never dream of taking such long chances with you, his friend, as to allow the subject to attempt actual murder. Then he hands the subject a revolver loaded with real ammunition.

What would happen? No one knows, for the experiment has never been tried. Erickson has approximated it with negative results; but the writer strongly suspects his findings are due to the attitude of the operator. Erickson is emphatic that hypnotism cannot be used in crime, and that subjects are uncanny in their ability to pick up this attitude. Wells and Roland would disagree with him. Personally, from what the writer knows of hypnotism he would not allow the experiment to be made on himself for any consideration whatever. It is his opinion that murder would be committed.

Of course, the reader can lodge a very obvious objection. The subject has not committed a murder in the real sense of the word. He was tricked into manslaughter, if we wish; he did not really commit murder. But this is a very practical world. We would, of course, remove from the subject all knowledge of ever having been hypnotized and render it impossible for anyone else to throw him in the trance. All he could tell the jury would be that he had an irresistible impulse to kill a man, which would only mean an institution for the criminal insane rather than the electric chair.

Would he still be unable to recall the incident when under trial conditions, when his life was actually in danger? Would the hypnotic suggestions still hold in such a situation? Once again, no one knows. But take the following case, which is much more to the point so far as warfare is concerned and which also eliminates the last objection.

We wish to blow up a munitions factory, so we pick on one especially good subject to "turn the trick." We rehearse him very carefully, pointing out that he is really doing very important work for the Federal Bureau of Investigation and run him through a number of fake experiments such as the one about to be described. All these end harmlessly, and we pay him well for his co-operation. In this way we both assure ourselves that he is the subject we want and assure him there is nothing to fear.

We then put him to the crucial test. We explain that the authorities must see what would happen in a real situation. We tell him we are putting a bomb in his dinner pail timed to explode two hours after he enters the plant in question. There is nothing to fear, for while the bomb looks genuine from the outside we have replaced the explosive with a harmless compound. He is to enter the factory as usual the next day and behave quite normally, for the authorities will be watching his every move.

Then we place in the dinner pail a genuine bomb timed to explode one half hour after he enters the plant. Would we succeed? A very open question but the writer, for one, would certainly not enter that plant on the morning in question if he could possibly avoid it. He will not say he is certain the trick would work; but he feels there is a very good chance of its success. And in this particular case there would be no one to question after the disaster.

We have outlined those obvious possible uses of hypnotism in warfare which would occur to anyone familiar with that branch of psychology. Needless to say we are not giving away military secrets any more than is a chemist who discourses on the use of gas or a physicist who talks on the magnetic mine. There are certain broad principles well known to everyone familiar with the field of chemistry, physics or psychology. Certain highly technical devices, however, are known only to the expert and to disclose these would be treason and punishable as such. We are merely stating the obvious, though in a field with which the average reader is much less familiar than he is with those of chemistry or physics.

We might expand on the suggestions we have already made to an almost infinite degree. During World War I, one leading authority on hypnotism offered to take a German submarine, piloted by a German commander under hypnosis, through the German mine fields and attack the German fleet. Whether he succeeded or not, his chance of returning was about zero: so we must at least credit him with the courage of his convictions. We could tell of other proposals which sound equally weird to the layman, but which might work.

Strangest of all perhaps in this strange picture is the danger of "counter-mining," of setting a trap for the hypnotist and literally blowing him into "kingdom come" with his own device. Let us cite a laboratory experiment by way of illustration. The writer would guarantee to take a good hypnotic subject and defy the best man in America to detect that he is acting under posthypnotic suggestion. That sounds like a large order but it would probably succeed.

For example, we choose a very good subject and then let him in on the plot. We disclose to him that he is an excellent hypnotic subject and we wish to use him for counterespionage. We suspect that in the near future someone is going to try hypnosis on him. He is to bluff, to co-operate to the very best of his ability, fake every test that is made and stay wide awake all the time. The test we fear most is that of an analgesia—insensitivity to pain. So we coach him carefully with posthypnotic suggestions to the effect that even when wide awake and bluffing he will be able to meet every test which may be made here, be it with ammonia under the nose, a needle, or, worst of all, the use of electricity, which can be made extremely painful, and is easy to use.

Under these circumstances it will be virtually impossible to tell whether this man is bluffing or really in trance. We take a subject so trained and allow another operator to try his hand. So the operator "hypnotizes" his victim and has him see the usual dog, produces anaesthesia to pin tricks, and is very well satisfied with himself. Then he "awakens" the subject.

We say to the operator. "That chap is a very good subject."

"He certainly is."

"He wouldn't have been fooling?"

"Not the least chance of it."

We turn to the subject, "What do you say?"

"I'm afraid I was. I remember everything perfectly. I was bluffing you."

The other operator now realizes he was "taken for a ride." So he returns to the attack. "Let's see you fool me *this* time."

He hynotizes the subject, stretches him out between two

chairs, sits on his chest and says triumphantly, "Now tell me he's fooling."

"That's right, I am." And the subject opens his eyes, dumps the operator on the floor and stands up.

"How in the world can I tell when you are hypnotized," says the very puzzled hypnotist.

"You can't. I know every trick of the trade and can bluff you from now till doomsday."

And he could have. This particular subject was almost uncanny. Highly intelligent, he knew all the literature on hypnotism and knew also exactly what was expected in every situation. At times the writer himself did not know what it was all about, whether the subject was bluffing or in genuine trance, for he could use autosuggestion quite as easily as the operator could use real hypnotism. He thoroughly enjoyed the whole game, and took especial delight in "playing possum." He would allow an operator to work with him for an hour under the absolute conviction that he was handling a high grade subject, and never crack a smile during the whole performance.

Of course this was a very excellent subject; but a "plant" carefully coached to meet just such a situation, and such a prepared subject would be a nightmare to any intelligence department using hypnotism. The writer is quite frank in admitting that he knows of no way to uncover the deception. Babinski, writing years ago, put his finger on this flaw. He declared there was no way to determine whether the subject was bluffing. With our more modern techniques we can be quite certain than an ordinary subject is genuine. We can apply a pain test which no one could stand outside the trance. But these specially prepared subjects are quite another matter. With posthypnotic suggestion they can be trained to meet very severe pain while quite "normal."

Under the conditions of warfare they would be a constant source of danger. The enemy, suspecting that we were using hypnotism, would "plant" a dozen or so subjects where he felt most certain we would find them. He would then stand an excellent chance of getting the inside track of the whole organization.

But after all, this is a problem with which the Intelligence Department is continually faced, the danger of a double cross, of some one selling out to a higher bidder. Given time and care, the writer is certain this menace could be reduced to a stage where it would be much less dangerous than in the ordinary practices of intelligence. While it is certainly a weak point in the entire technique of using hypnotism in warfare it gives us not the least excuse to reject this device. When we do reject it we hand the enemy a weapon which may be just as deadly as poison gas and admit that we cannot meet him on equal terms.

That, it seems to the writer, is one great danger with which we are faced in the present world situation. We may easily take that "holier-than-thou" attitude, and say that such practices are all very well for our barbarian enemy but we will never stoop to these means. All of which is, of course nonsense. Every innovation in war is brutal. We read that in the old days when gunpowder was just coming in, it was common practice for many of these good old knights to strike off the hands of musketeers when these were captured, and Bayard, the knight whose name is a byword for courage and honor, skinned alive the first enemy gunpowder user he captured. The use of gas by the Germans in World War I was heralded as an act of unqualified barbarism, but the British later knighted the man who invented mustard gas, and we Americans manufactured millions of cubic feet of it.

The aeroplane is another and later nightmare. There are many who wish that the Wright brothers had made sail-boats their hobby, but they didn't. Now we can say what we wish, but both sides will use the bomber in the way best calculated to win any war. Parachute troops were a blot against international law, and the British said so. Later, they and we tried to outparachute the original parachutists.

War is brutal in its very essence. Even should we still regard it as a glorified cricket match and refuse to use such a novel device as hypnotism we must at least protect ourselves against its use by others. For those others may have no such scruples, and in the last analysis hypnotism is no more unethical than gas, bombs—or than war as a whole, so far as that goes.

The British have paid a terrible price for refusing to look reality in the face. We might easily do the same if we became over squeamish in our determination to protect ourselves ethically. We may rest assured that certain world powers will not hesitate one moment to use hypnotism directly they are convinced of its value. Then it will be incumbent on us to beat them at their own game, but under these circumstances the hand of the military must not be tied by any silly prejudices in the minds of the general public. War is the end of all law. When we speak of keeping within the rules of the game we are childish, because it is not a game and the rules never hold. In the last analysis any device is justifiable which enables us to protect ourselves from defeat.

Chapter IX

HYPNOTISM AND HITLERISM

A S the reader will recall, we have several times made the statement that Hitler was the world's best hypnotist. Moreover, we said that we were not playing on words. We can best understand Hitler's success by understanding hypnotism, which is merely exaggerated suggestibility. One psychologist defined a suggestion as "the acceptance of a proposition in the absence of logically adequate proof." Let us take an example which may apply to any one of us in the next five years, and work back to our explanation from that.

You are seated in front of your fire on an evening with your thoughts centered on the latest best seller. Your neighbor, Graves, arrives for a friendly chat. He is quite calm and mentions that another of your neighbors, Smith, has come in for a little gossip lately. It appears that his name was Schmidt before he changed it and that he was born in Germany. You like Smith even if he once was Schmidt. Besides, you are very comfortable and don't wish to be disturbed. Graves mentions the fact that Smith is suspected of being a German spy, but Graves is not at all excited, and you let the matter drop there.

This is situation number one. Note very carefully what happens next when we hear more rumors or facts concerning Schmidt and proceed to whip up your emotions, in other words to use suggestion. Two hours later Graves returns. He has obviously been drinking and is very excited. He has heard again that this man Schmidt—alias Smith—is a German spy. We are at war with Germany. Graves has a son in the army. So have you. Why wait until this man has a chance to do his dirty work. Let's go over to his house, take him out, and lynch him!

Now, what happens? That depends pretty largely on you. Probably when you realize that Graves has been drinking and that Schmidt is likely to be the victim of gossip you try to quiet Graves' obsessions, but if you are one of those individuals who is highly suggestible himself, if you belong to the "one-in-five" club he may very easily convert you to his point of view and the two of you set off to arouse the town.

You may, of course, be one of those people who are "negatively" suggestible, who react contrary to all suggestions. In this case you will do your best to argue with Graves, to point out to him the fact that he has no real basis for his suspicions and that the whole matter is one for the police. You might even call up the authorities after he has left and warn them that Schmidt may need police protection.

But you are probably one of those individuals who likes to be fair-minded and also likes to keep out of trouble. The chances are you will decline to go with Graves and simply sit at home confused and worried over the whole affair.

Now let us go along to situation number three. Two hours later you hear a tremendous commotion across the street. Graves has been successful and a mob of fifty men have assembled in front of Schmidt's house intent on lynching him. You rush out to see what it is all about, and ask the first member of the mob what is happening.

"This man Schmidt is a German spy. We are going to lynch him."

"How do you know he's a spy?"

"Everyone says so. Come on. Let's get him."

Now what do you do? As you read this book you are convinced you would rush to the front and beg that howling mob to use reason. But probably you would do no such thing. A mob is a very ugly proposition. It needs a very brave man to stand in the way of one of these emotional avalanches, and few of us have the courage. Experience shows that you probably will hang around the edge of the mob, feeling very unhappy with everything but making no actual attempt to stop the lynching.

Then something curious is very liable to happen. You slowly become interested in that mob. After all, you are an American, you have a son in the army. Schmidt was born in Germany. Why shouldn't he be a spy? Everyone says so and who are you to combat the will of the group. Your open hostility to the mob changes to acquiescence. They can do what they wish, so far as you are concerned.

Study of these situations shows us that the next step is liable to follow in very short order. Your passive acquiescence changes to active participation. You yourself become one of the mob and are just as determined to bring Schmidt to a summary justice as is any other member of the group. Quietly reading this book, such a statement may seem absurd, but we can assure you it is anything but absurd. The mob has a fatal habit of engulfing those who come merely as passive spectators.

Why? Let us look at the actual working of your own mind as you leave the house to reason with that group of angry men. Emotion is one great sensitizer of the human brain and so leaves the individual very open to suggestion. You suddenly plunge yourself into a highly emotional situation.

The first emotion to make itself felt, if you wish to interfere, will be plain fear. If you attempt to thwart that mob you do so at the risk of your own life, and there are not many people in this world who will gamble their lives to oppose a group of their own friends and neighbors. On the other hand, you may realize that you should do just that thing. You are torn betwixt duty and fear, a very upsetting emotional state.

But there is another peculiarity of emotion which will tend to make you, the innocent bystander, more suggestible and may very easily drag you into the mob. This we term emotional contagion. Emotions are as contagious as measles. We see this clearly in any social situation. At the movies we laugh together, weep at the same time or all become patriotic when we see the flag. If we see a group of men laughing before a store window we are probably smiling very broadly before we have the least idea what is in that window. Should we see another group collected on the road and looking very serious we will suspect an accident and will not approach that group, ourselves, prepared to burst into laughter.

This fact of emotional contagion is very important in mob psychology. More than one writer on the subject has noted how easily the mob absorbed into itself the stranger who certainly had nothing in common with that mob and might never see its members again in all his life.

It is very difficult in dealing with this question of the mob and its high suggestibility to say which of certain factors come first. One very important factor, however, which probably helps emotional contagion is that which we term restriction of the field of consciousness. In normal life we are always attending to many things at once. This does not allow any one stimulus to monopolize our attention. But in the mob we are attending to only one thing for there is nothing else to distract our attention. The roaring of the mob, or the wild exhortations of the leader are effective in blotting out every other stimulus.

The result is clear. One train of suggestions and only one fall on the ears of the listener. He already has his emotions aroused, so he is hyper-suggestible. These suggestions he is now receiving are also highly emotional in character. As a result we have that peculiar "avalanching" of emotional fury which we see in the mob. The more suggestible, the more emotional; the more emotional, the more suggestible, a terribly vicious circle which can easily get out of hand and cause great trouble.

The writer was visiting a small American town in the north one New Year's Eve. Everything seemed quite normal. At the head of Main Street the crowd became rough. Perhaps the police were not as tactful as they might have been but it is all very obscure. The crowd started breaking windows, the police interfered, and the fat was in the fire. The mob thoroughly "beat up" two policemen and raged through half a mile of that town smashing and looting according to very best mob traditions. Only a detachment of regular troops finally got the situation in hand. The next morning both the town, the authorities and the mob members were completely puzzled as to what had really occurred.

In another city the writer was present when a lynching occurred. It was the usual story of a white woman insulted by a negro. The crowd went wild, wrecked the negro quarter and finally hanged the culprit to a lamp-post. Unfortunately, it was not the culprit but a man who, as later investigation showed, could not possibly have been associated with the crime in question. But the mob had its way and the man was dead as might have been anyone, white or black, who interefered with that group at the height of its fury.

Restriction of the field of consciousness and emotional contagion undoubtedly are very important factors in determining the high suggestibility—hypnotizibility, if you will—of the mob. It is difficult to say which precedes the other, whether the high emotion tends to restrict the field of consciousness or vice versa. But once we have our mob well under way there are two other factors which tend to give it that irresistible fury so characteristic of these groups.

One of these we term social sanction. Man is a social animal. As one authority puts it, every situation is a social situation. We simply must conform to some group somewhere. That group may even be an ideal one and have no real existence, but to the average man the group is not ideal but very real. His religious sect, his political party, perhaps his secret fraternity command his loyalty. He is very dependent upon the opinion of this group and will go a long way to have his conduct conform to its ideals.

In the mob he suddenly finds himself in another group and here, as a member of that group, he acts under group sanction. He has the feeling of omnipotence. Everyone within sight agrees that he should hang Smith or that he should join the marines. In his highly emotional and suggestible state of mind he is quite willing to do either. This "group sanction" is all that is necessary to turn the scales and he acts accordingly.

The final factor we would call to the reader's attention in considering the mob is the removal of inhibitions, a result of the three factors already mentioned. The individual, highly suggestible, in a storm of emotion and acting with the approval of the group will commit acts of which he would never dream in a more normal state. Destruction of property, looting, even murder are all familiar phenomena to those who have studied mob activity. Yet take almost any member of that mob, propose to him individually after a good meal that he break a plate glass window, steal a fur coat or murder his neighbor and he would recoil in horror. Man does not do that sort of thing unless he is acting under the influence of suggestion or perhaps of certain drugs. At any rate, he is not normal according to his own higher standards.

Let us now note the very close resemblance between the psychology of the mob and the factors underlying hypnotism. Both emotion and hypnotism sensitize the brain. There is one large school of thought in psychology which would claim hypnotism or exaggerated suggestibility to be simply an emotional state, that the suggestion we get as a result of high emotion is identical with that which we obtain from hypnotism. In this school of thought we would find the psychoanalysts and many others who cannot agree with psychoanalysis in all its teachings. We ourselves agree with their viewpoint and claim that the study of hypnotism is one excellent way of approaching mob psychology.

Take the five factors we have outlined as the essentials of mob psychology. First, an appeal to the emotions by prestige or direct suggestion. To the writer there can be no doubt that we do the same in hypnotism. This is not quite so evident in the laboratory technique, perhaps, but is clearly seen in the approach

of the stage hypnotist. His whole technique consists in throwing his subject off balance emotionally and then following up
his advantage before the victim has a chance to regain his
composure.

The writer once had one of these professionals as his guest.
Several students who were majors in psychology came around
to make his acquaintance. They asked him to demonstrate and
he demonstrated one or two simple tests which located for him
a couple of good subjects. Then the real demonstration began.
These men knew that, in theory, he could not hypnotize them
without their consent, and were inclined to be a little con-
temptuous of this illiterate stage hypnotist, illiterate in that he
was a "show man" and knew nothing whatsoever of academic
psychology. This attitude nettled the visitor and he decided
a lesson was in order.

Approaching one of those he had decided were good subjects,
he made the blunt announcement, "I'm going to hypnotize you."

"Thanks. I don't want to be hypnotized."

"That doesn't mean a thing," replied the professional. He
stepped up quickly in front of his victim, seized him by both
arms, looked straight in his eyes and said, "Now, listen, my
child, I'm going to give you a little lesson in manners. You
can't take your eyes off mine, so don't waste time in trying.
And you can't sit down in the chair, so stand where you are.
You are going sound sleep. I will count to five. By the time I
get to five you will be out on your feet."

And he was. The subject was obviously angry, made abortive
efforts to strike the hypnotist but went into a deep trance, a very
neat display of the highly emotional nature of the "professional"
attack. If any of our readers will take the opportunity of watching the stage performer work on his subject for the first time,
they will see clearly what we mean. He does not "play around,"
but goes right to the point with a direct, domineering, frontal
attack. Such an approach is highly unpleasant to most people
and awakens strong emotions, closely akin to fear or anger.

This, of course, plays directly into the hypnotist's hands. The emotion sensitizes the brain so that his suggestions then become irresistible.

This emotional factor is not quite so apparent in the psychologist's laboratory but the elements are present. The average individual approaches an hypnotic experiment with mixed feelings, generally curiosity and some slight degree of fear. With certain individuals this emotional outlook is more to the fore than with others and it seems probable that these people turn out to be the really good subjects. Why these particular subjects should react with high emotion while others do not is a point in theory which is beyond the scope of this book.

After this direct appeal to emotion, which if successful makes the individual highly suggestible, we have as our next step in mob psychology a restriction of the field of consciousness. It is difficult to say whether this precedes or follows emotional contagion but we will presume it comes first. This is of fundamental importance to success in hypnotism as well. All our techniques aim at confining the subject's attention to some one very limited field. The early "mesmerist" accomplished this end by having the subject look in his eyes while he further held his attention by a series of impressive passes.

Braid, working in the 1840's, used the trick of having his subjects concentrate on some bright object generally held in a position where it put a slight strain on the eyes. This technique reached its culmination in the mirror of Lys, a rotating mirror which continually flashed a light into the subject's eyes, so serving to hold his attention while the operator made his suggestions.

The professional on the stage accomplishes the same end with his direct, domineering attack, trusting to hold the subject's attention by this method, while the psychologist in his laboratory strives toward the same end with a somewhat different technique. Quiet and monotonous repetition are the keynotes of his "sleeping" technique. "You are falling sound asleep,

sound asleep. You are going deeper and deeper. Your limbs
are tired, your elbows and knees feel tired. You are falling
sound asleep." He repeats this formula world without end, trusting that his voice will monopolize the subject's attention and
restrict the field of consciousness.

Thus we see another point of close resemblance between the
psychology of the mob and the psychology of suggestion or
hypnotism. The reader will bear with us as we follow through
this line of attack, for once we have established the very close
relationship between the two we will be in a position to really
understand the secret of Hitler's power or of most other great
public figures either of our own day or as described for us
in history.

Emotional contagion we find in hypnotism as we do in the
mob although it is not quite so evident from one viewpoint.
From another, however, it is even more so. We can deliberately
suggest to a subject any emotion whatsoever and, in many
cases we will have it faithfully reflected. The writer saw one instance where this had very sad results for one of the spectators.
An hypnotist in the army was giving a very good demonstration
before a group of officers. His subject, a sergeant, was a power-
fully built chap with a perpetual grouch. This sergeant was
particularly allergic to a certain Major X. So the hypnotist,
to add a touch of comedy, selected one of the group, a lowly
lieutenant, and whispered in the subject's ear that it was the
hated Major X.

The result was dramatic if not comic. The sergeant stepped
up to the lieutenant and let loose a barrage of profanity which
caused even the hard-boiled Canadian officers to gasp. Moreover, the aggrieved sergeant showed every intention of following the verbal attack with assault and battery before the hypnotist again had the situation under control.

It is a well-known fact that in hypnotism we can influence
the heart beat. This is most easily done by suggesting to the
subject some strong emotion, such as fear or anger. We always

suspect the individual in trance of bluffing, of putting on a show to satisfy the operator. But it is difficult to see how this play acting could effect heart beat, rate of breathing, or perspiration as shown on the psycho-galvanic reflex. It would seem much more reasonable to assume that the emotions suggested are genuine, a very excellent example of emotional contagion.

In fact, the writer doubts very much if even a Hitler can produce the savage anger he has seen obtained in some hypnotic subjects as a result of suggestion. It can be done very convincingly with the posthypnotic suggestion. We take a subject, a violent anti-Nazi, and suggest to him that Jones of the group belongs to the Bund. However, we also point out that we are having tea with Jones and he must behave like a gentleman.

This he does, within very broad limits. He is coldy discourteous, takes every possible opportunity to slur the Nazi and is obviously spoiling for a fight. But he does keep himself within bounds until the party breaks up. Then he is quite determined that he is going Jones' way, whichever way that may be. At this point, we remove the delusion and have Jones leave. For all that, the subject still has a "hang-over" and leaves the house breathing fury against everything that is not one hundred per cent American.

We also see in hypnotism as in the mob that feeling of omnipotence which comes from the social sanction, the approval of the crowd. Its origin to be sure is a little different when seen in hypnotism. Here the crowd is the hypnotist, for he is the only communication which the subject has with his surroundings. He is the only stimulating factor, at least the only one to which the subject gives any obvious attention.

And the hypnotist can, within certain broad limits, twist the subject around his finger as successfully as can any mob. These limits may be broad with some subjects, narrow with others, but within them the subject obviously feels that he has adequate social sanction. We see this reflected as a sort of mellowing of viewpoint when we talk to certain subjects.

For example, Young is a very rabid prohibitionist. In the waking state there are only two sides to this argument, his and the one that is wrong. In hypnotism, however, he became quite open-minded, although still holding his own view. We swing him by giving him the feeling of the group sanction.

"Oh, come now," we say, "You are a highly intelligent chap and this is the twentieth century. All your friends are very open-minded on this proposition. In fact, everybody feels that the prohibition law was a great mistake. You shouldn't be so dogmatic on these questions. Now, take Ayers, for example. He certainly is a very able man but he would never be dogmatic on any question."

Finally, he reaches the point where he is willing to argue the matter with much more light and much less heat, largely, we venture to say, because of emotional contagion and because of the feeling that his group sanctions a broader attitude. Just how much farther we could go in this particular case we do not know. The writer feels it is always unwise to press an issue beyond a certain point unless there is a definite end in view.

Lastly, in hypnotism, we can arrive at the dead end, the mob end, so to speak, where we get that removal of inhibitions which gives such a sinister aspect to mob action. To be sure, we do not dare go as far in the laboratory as the individual will go in the mob. This would involve the actual commission of crime which is impossible for reasons stated in the previous two chapters, but all the elements are present. The writer recalls his first acquaintance with hypnotism. He attended a stage exhibition and arrived late. He was horrified to see a respected acquaintance stripped to his underwear with a broom handle for a flute gamboling around the stage under the delusion that he was a Greek faun. Highly gratified also to see the faun knock the hypnotist flat the moment the trance was removed. This performance left a deep conviction in his mind that hypnotism was a very serious matter and had much deeper significance in many walks of life than most people realize.

The writer once hypnotized a soldier and had a very fine example of this removal of inhibition. This chap was a steady, reliable man who did his duty and gave no cause for complaint. He was in deep trance and the writer said, "Now, Mac, you're in good hands and no one cares what happens. Is there anything you would like to do?"

"There certainly is," said Mac, and he started swearing. He damned everything in the army from the general to the lowest private. Then he started on the Germans and gave them his undivided profane attention for fifteen minutes. Next he devoted his attention to the "slackers" at home, inventing several names for them which were new even to an army man. Suddenly he stopped.

"Thanks. I feel better."

"How about waking up?"

"Good idea. Snap me out of it."

Once awake he was obviously relieved by this terrific outburst. "You know," he said, "I never felt so well since this war started. Let's try it again some time."

This curious release of energy is quite familiar to the psychoanalyst. He calls it abreaction. We do not often obtain it in hypnotism unless we provoke the same. Then it seems to do the subject much good, a result we would expect from the psychoanalytic literature. If the reader should be interested in the relation between hypnotism and psychoanalysis we would advise Schilder's book, *Psychotherapy*, or the work by Schilder and Kauders, *Hypnosis*.

Let us now examine the technique of a Hitler or a Mussolini. We will note first that the attack is primarily aimed at the emotions. No leader of the "rabble rouser" type can hope to make any progress at all with a purely intellectual approach. To be sure, we do not often find the purely emotional attack emphasized to quite the extent we did in those modern dictators but it is always basic.

First, we have fear. It would be a brave man indeed in Germany or Italy of the war years who dared to raise his voice against the leader. Before the war, foreigners travelling in Italy always referred to Mussolini as Mr. Brown. So thorough were the secret police, so omnipresent that even the mention of the Italian fascist's name might very easily lead to an interview with the police. This was not so serious in the case of the tourist but was a very bad thing indeed for any native Italian. It was a well known fact that many people who dared voice open criticism of Mussolini simply vanished.

The Nazis improved very much on this technique. To instil genuine fear a concentration camp is much more effective. Death is a sudden thing and tends to be forgotten but the living death of a political prisoner is a constant reminder to all that discretion is preferable to courage. The stories we read in such books as *Out of the Night* (Jan Valtin) seem to be substantially correct. It is difficult for the American to imagine such happenings and at first we simply dismissed them with that very useful word "propaganda." However, we in this country are gradually learning that we have to learn a lot. Nothing is more difficult than the education of the educated, and our high standard of education told us that the dark ages ended some four hundred years ago. That seems to have been a mistake.

But fear, while a powerful emotion, is largely negative in its actions. It is a useful device with which to silence opposition, but a far more useful foundation on which to build. For hatred can have no better basis than fear, real or imagined, and hate is dynamic. With hatred of the Jews, of the French, of all democracies, we have an emotion which makes a people blindly open to all sorts of suggestion, and with which we can "go places." Add to this a myth of Nordic superiority, a fervid patriotism to the fatherland and we have that peculiar brand of dynamite we called Nazi Germany.

Let us not underestimate its power. The fanatic has cut a bloody path through the pages of history. The voice of reason, of temperance can no more stop his progress than a flimsy dam turn aside a raging torrent. We will quote a couple of very interesting illustrations. One of the best known German psychologists actually published a work showing that Nordic hens are superior to Mediterranean hens. This work was the purest trash so far as science is concerned, but was terribly potent if fed to an inflamed people.

Moreover, it is a startling example of what the sheer power of fear can do to the scientific mind. The psychologist in question can have had no delusions as to the weakness of his case—and no delusions as to his own fate should he refuse to obey orders. It was simply a case of "play ball—or else." While we may condemn this attitude from a safe seat in a democratic country it is well to bear in mind that we are taking an academic view of things, while he was faced with a very grim reality.

Another interesting case refers to a certain man, a composer, of non-Aryan stock. His works sold well and, for financial reasons, it was very much in the interests of the Nazis to have him in the country as a satisfied citizen. Any individual with more than seventy-five per cent Aryan blood is officially an Aryan. So they analyzed his blood and made the discovery that he had seventy-six per cent of the desired blood in his veins. There is no test known to science by which we can tell Aryan blood from Mediterranean or Jewish, but that is quite beside the point. Such results, published with the stamp of official approval, are just as true, just as potent as a genuine scientific statement in so far as they count in arousing public opinion.

Next, we find that Hitler used two more factors already mentioned in hypnotism and in mob psychology with consummate skill. These were restriction of the fields of attention and emotional contagion. Time played into his hands here. Never before in the history of the world did we have devices, such as our modern press and radio, with which an entire people can be reached. If, now, we establish control over press and radio we have a tremendously potent weapon. We can restrict the field of attention to such topics as we choose. The citizen in his home was allowed no distraction from the one dominant theme, Nordic superiority. This was buttressed in every possible way with a direct appeal to the very strongest of his emotions, fear, hatred, and anger.

No hypnotist could ask for a better approach. A highly sensitized brain, one theme song pushed home day and night. Emotional contagion is a foregone conclusion. Those few individuals who have the courage to question the authorities are segregated in concentration camps. Those who dare turn the radio to short wave and pick up foreign stations do so at great risk to themselves. Those few who have access to foreign papers and dare read these are taking even greater chances. We doubt if any hypnotist seeking group hypnotism could perfect a better approach than that adopted by the German leader. It certainly is incomparably superior to that possessed by a Caesar or a Napoleon. To be sure, it is largely an accident of time and mechanical invention, but that does not in any way detract from its ghastly efficiency.

This control of radio and press gives the dictator another distinct advantage when he wishes to whip up the emotions of his people and play on these. In a democracy such as ours it is necessary to educate public opinion before the government can take drastic steps. We see this clearly in the very slow awakening of the United States and Great Britain to their danger. It is all very well to condemn our leaders for the state of unpreparedness in which we found ourselves. We have to blame someone and we always condemn the government on general principles. But we know perfectly well that a Chamberlain or a Roosevelt who had foreseen the emergency and had dared to advocate a proper rearmament program would have been branded as a war-monger and might very easily have been expelled from office.

The dictator has an incomparable advantage. He controls press and radio. so he can determine what line of action he is to follow, what suggestions are to be given his hypnotized subjects. The results are exactly what we see in the hypnotic trance. He can "reverse his field" at a minute's notice. With hypnotism we can have the subject weeping at one moment, laughing a minute later and very angry in five minutes more.

So Hitler whipped up in his people an almost fanatical hatred for the Russians for five years, then suddenly changed his tactics completely. Over night he shifted his ground. The Russians are splendid people. It is really the Poles who are the great menace—and his people accepted this as the hypnotized subject does any hypnotic suggestion, which is exactly what it was.

Then, overnight, it was again the Russians.

We can readily imagine the chaos in this country if during the war the President had suddenly announced that our real friends were the Japs, that we agreed to let them have Australia and the East Indies, while it was our obvious duty, because of American superiority, to take over Canada and Mexico at once, with a "protectorate" over all the Latin American countries—until we could really absorb them.

Yet this is exactly what a dictator can and could do. Mussolini managed to stop Hitler in Austria. For six years Hitler had been blasting away at the Russians. The League blocked Mussolini in Ethiopia. Overnight he and the Italian people became ardent admirers of Hitler, and the Germans suddenly discovered that the Russians were at least near-Aryan, if not quite pure. Later, of course, they became a slave race once more.

We wish to emphasize the fact that this astounding control is just as much hypnotic as that ever exercised in any laboratory. It depends on direct prestige suggestion registering on a brain highly sensitized by emotion. That is about as good a description of hypnotism as we can have. To be sure, the techniques are slightly different, but no different from the techniques employed by various hypnotists. Watch the psychologist working quietly in his laboratory, carefully avoiding all noise and distraction. Now switch over to the stage hypnotist. "The

brighter the lights, the bigger the crowd, the better the success."
We point out that Adolf Hitler haranguing his audience in
the glare of stage lighting had more in common with the "professional" than this latter has with the laboratory psychologist.
We simply have not, up to now, realized how very similar were
the two techniques.

If the reader will recall the various pictures of Hitler in his
speeches, he will note that on more than one occasion the German leader resorted to an excellent hypnotic device. He staged
the meeting at night in the open. He himself stood in the
glare of lights, above his audience, forcing the listeners to look
up and at a bright object. Braid in the 1840's discovered that
this simple concentration on an object was quite enough to get
hypnotism and was the first to popularize the technique.

It is very important that we realize the close resemblance
between the technique of giving suggestions—in other words,
hypnotism as used by a mob leader and that employed on the
stage. The writer recalls a boyhood experience. Very frequently,
when we recall such early events they shed light on more adult
problems and cause us to investigate farther. He was attending
one of those old fashioned revival meetings which were, if
nothing else, an emotional workout. One of his friends was quite
carried away by the oratory, the singing and the emotional
atmosphere. He was converted, went up to the "sinners' seat"
and was numbered among the lowest. It afterward struck the
writer as curious that the convert's recollection seemed very
hazy. He had to be told what happened from then on.

Later when the writer became more interested in hypnotism
he did some further inquiries on the subject. In a considerable
proportion of these cases, such as those seen at the famous
"camp meetings" the convert does seem to be in more or less
of a trance during the whole procedure. His memory is hazy
and his conduct certainly irrational as in "treeing the devil"
wherein the penitents chase his satanic majesty up a tree and sit
barking around the base. In fact there are few better examples

of mass hypnotism than these old revival services and it is very important that we recognize them for what they are. We are all too prone to adopt the "holier-than-thou" attitude. These things very naturally occur in a country like Germany or Italy. We are not so willing to admit that man is man the world over; that some of our best examples of mob hysteria are to be found right here in America.

A brother psychologist reports the following experience which may add a further illustration to our line of argument. One evening he was literally at the corner drugstore of a college town. A truck drove up, the sides folded down in a platform and under the intense light of powerful reflectors a high pressure salesman proceeded to sell his wares. His plea, apparently was that he was a good sport, the audience were good sports and that he was going to prove it.

First came the old trick of selling fifty cent pieces for a quarter. This proved him to be a good sport. Then he raised the ante, and sold dollar bills for fifty cents. All the time under the glare of those lights up on his truck he kept up a constant barrage of suggestions on his audience. They were good sports, he was a good sport, all Americans were good sports, down with all dictators. The show went on for half an hour. He was selling his audience two dollar bills for one dollar.

Then an amazing thing happened. He produced the real reason for his presence, namely fountain pens. Moreover, he was quite honest. The pens cost him fifty cents each. He was selling them for five dollars each, but he needed the money badly and they were as good as any other pen. He had been a good sport. Now how many would buy his pens for five dollars each. They sold like wild fire! Moreover, many of the purchasers were people who certainly could not afford such a luxury and according to the narrator, were acting in a daze.

Finally came the proper climax. The salesman suddenly ended his harangue. Three men, described by this colleague as being the toughest looking chaps he had ever seen put in an

appearance, the truck folded up and the whole outfit was gone in
five minutes. They were taking no chances on that mob suddenly
waking up and discovering what it was all about. As neat an
example of group hypnotism as one could wish. Bright lights,
high emotion, restriction of the field of consciousness. Even
Hitler could not have done better.

Finally let us note the last two phenomena characteristic of
mob psychology and of hypnotism. These are the feeling of
omnipotence largely due to the social sanction and the release
of inhibitions. The dictator can build up this illusion of the
social sanction in splendid form through his controlled radio
and press. The Nordics were the only superior race, they were
being hemmed in and persecuted by all other groups but it was
their God-given duty to rise superior to these circumstances
and rule the world.

Such a line of attack gives the individual the necessary social
sanction for his actions, also supplies that feeling of omnipotence so necessary to group action. He is acting with the full
approval of his group, the only group which is worthy of any
consideration. Therefore, any action he undertakes at the be-
quest of this group is justified. This gives him sanction for the
release of all inhibitions. Nothing succeeds like excess, to quote
Cutten. The most amazing thing in the rise of Hitler and his
fellow dictators is the lengths to which people can go.

Great emotional storms, examples of group hypnotism have
swept this world many times in the course of its history. Mohammed was one of those great leaders who could arouse man
and send him forth to do or die and the Christian answer to
Mohammed was the Crusades. These we can more or less
understand, but the famous Children's Crusade lacks even the
vestige of reason. The bitterness with which man will fight his
brother when once aroused is without parallel in the animal
kingdom for no where else do we have even an approach to
war among all nature's millions of species.

The Reformation is a classic and terrible example, not only

in the bitter strife between Protestant and Catholic, but the equally deadly hatred among the various Protestant sects. It would be childish to claim that all this strife was on reasonable and logical ground. Invariably it can be traced to the dynamic leadership of some one individual who doubtlessly was in most cases quite convinced that his interpretation of God's will was correct. Unfortunately in most of these cases, as modern psychology could point out, the leader was definitely abnormal, neurotic or even insane. But that cannot recall to life the thousands who died as the result of his teachings.

If, now we examine Hitler, we will see that his fatal genius held to the line of most great leaders who have led humanity nowhere through a sea of blood. His basic appeal was absolutely non-logical. The thesis of Nordic superiority is pure trash if we consult science. Many fine books have been written on the races of man by careful scholars. Some of these races, such as the native Australian, the Ainu or the Andamanese, are being rapidly exterminated. Research shows us that it is the disease germ which is largely responsible. It has been demonstrated more than once that these people are just as "intelligent" as the white man, but immunity to smallpox, diphtheria or cholera has little to do with intelligence.

Hatred of the Jew was another keystone of Hitler's emotional appeal. But the Jew was highly civilized when the illiterate Germans, English and French were settling their endless feuds with their stone clubs and spears. Moreover, for the last two thousand years the Jew has been pretty much international. The Romans were never particularly gentle when it came to dealing with dangerous minorities. They spent three centuries, off and on, in a savage and ruthless slaughter of the Christians. Strange to say, they got on very nicely with the Jew, as have most other nations up to this present century. To be sure, there has been a certain amount of persecution. Sometimes, as in the case of Spain, it does not make very pleasant reading. The Jew has no army, does have money. When a government needs a scapegoat to cloak its own inefficiency it has always been safe—and profitable—to single out the Jew. But for all that, we doubt if the Jew has led as miserable a life as has the average French-man, German or Italian. The wars of the ages have mostly passed him by and his economic position has on the whole been above the average.

The Treaty of Versailles,—we might say that here Hitler did have the basis of a just complaint. But he tore up that treaty with the consent of both France and England. At the time of his invasion of Czechoslovakia every point in the treaty was either settled or on its way to solution. The Polish corridor was no fighting matter and England under Chamberlain the appeaser, would doubtlessly have given him satisfaction on the matter of colonies. In fact, we may safely say that at the time of the Czech invasion Hitler had unwritten the Treaty of Versailles. He might easily have become Europe's greatest statesman, creating both a United States of Europe and a new world order without shedding a drop of blood.

But, as one writer puts it "that sort of genius does not have that sort of genius." The mob leader rapidly learns that he must appeal to emotion, not to reason. Moreover, it is much easier to use hate and fear as the hypnotic, than love and understand-ing. For, if we appeal to love, as did Christ, reason is the necessary correlate. If we appeal to hate or fear, then reason becomes our worst enemy. The mob leader gets caught in a hopeless and vicious circle. He achieves his end by playing on man's lowest emotions. These "cruel, brutal and destructive" instincts cannot be satisfied. Their very nature must become more and more all consuming, the fires must burn ever more fiercely. Hitler could no more have curbed his followers' thirst for power and revenge than can a hungry tiger restrain himself in the presence of a lamb.

All this we can best understand by a close study of the laws of suggestion, in other words, hypnotism. The psychologist in his laboratory, the "professional" on the stage, the demagogue haranguing the mob all use essentially the same technique, attack by direct or prestige suggestion on a mind sensitized by emotion. We must learn to recognize the fact that, from the psychologist's point of view, many successful orators are simply high grade hypnotists.

Chapter X

CONCLUSIONS

HYPNOTISM is a particular form of direct or prestige suggestion, something to which we are all exposed every day of our lives. The reader will, in general, be familiar with two types of hypnotism, that used by the psychologist in his laboratory, that used by the stage performer, the "professional." The writer would call attention to a third type of direct suggestion, not generally classed as hypnotism. The orator, in general, be he on the radio or directly addressing an audience uses all the psychological tricks of the hypnotist and gets most of the results achieved by the latter. In fact, his technique has more in common with the "professional" than has the stage performer's with that of the laboratory psychologist.

To be sure, the orator does not get the trance, but we know that neither trance nor loss of consciousness is necessary in regular hypnotism to obtain all our phenomena. Certain other conditions, as anaesthesia, hallucinations or paralyses are not common with the orator, although we get all of them in certain religious groups. On the other hand, other phenomena, such as delusions are far more common in the mob or the crowd than in ordinary hypnosis. For example we might say with scientific accuracy that the two outstanding characteristics of the present day dictator are delusions of grandeur and delusions of persecution. These he imparts to his followers with no more logical backing than has the subject in hypnotic trance when we tell him he is Abraham Lincoln or George Washington. The writer stresses this point because, to him, the great orator is generally a great hypnotist using direct or prestige suggestion with far more skill than the psychologist employs when he works with

228

hypnotic suggestion. In general, his appeal will be on an emotional, non-logical basis since this sensitizes the brain and gives his suggestions far greater strength than can be obtained with any logical appeal.

For this reason an understanding of hypnotism is of immense importance to the average layman. Taken by itself it presents a fascinating picture. The hallucinations, paralyses, automatic movements, posthypnotic suggestions and autosuggestions are naturally of great interest to any reader. But they are just what they are, and of no more practical importance than the description of a surgical operation for appendicitis. In fact, they are of less importance.

But taken as a background from which to understand the human being, his weird excesses in religion and in war, taken as the basis of mob psychology, these phenomena of hypnotism immediately assume an importance as great as any presented by other fields of science. The engineer designs his aeroplane with consummate skill. To the people of the world at this present day the fact of the aeroplane has little importance but the use to which it will be put is something very different. The average citizen of London will never travel in one of those sky birds but he has no delusions as to what they can do when put in the hands of a ruthless adversary. We can only understand the working of Hitler's mind and his power over others as we understand the psychology of suggestion, to which hypnotism is our best approach.

A brief survey of hypnotism as hypnotism impresses us more with the rigidity of human thought than with the brilliance of the human mind. A Mesmer, a Braid or a Bernheim has courage enough to do a little independent thinking, A dull senseless opposition of prejudice and inertia, both in the medical and the lay world, holds grimly to the brakes of progress. But, after all, hypnotism is not here in a class by itself. The whole history of human thought warns that the original thinker had "better be good" and tough otherwise his days will be none too happy.

But the history of hypnotism also shows us that, given time, the human mind will insist on the truth. Mesmer, back in the 1770's advanced his crude fallacious theories, but he opened a great field to investigation. Benjamin Franklin, certainly no hidebound conservative, assisted in running him out of Paris. One hundred years later we find Charcot and Binet still supporting his views, great original thinkers in their own fields but utterly blind to progress in others. Liebeault and Bernheim finally disposed of that very persistent ghost, animal magnetism. Then from 1880 to almost 1930 hypnotism went through another resting stage, crowded out in large part by the work of one more original thinker, S. Freud, founder of the psychoanalytical school.

Now we find hypnotism again in the field of active research. Strange to say, many of its most active opponents come from the ranks of our most liberal profession, medicine. Yet it was these same doctors who, fifty years ago gave hypnotism a respectable standing in the realm of science. Truly we live in a weird world. When now the psychologist proposes to carry his research into the field of education, of crime, even of warfare, we may expect the usual uproar from both layman and even professional psychologist.

These truths should not be discussed in public. They are too dangerous, too mysterious, in fact too anything in this broad wide world if only we will let sleeping dogs lie. But science never was and never can be concerned with the possible, even probably, mal-usage of its discoveries. Science seeks truth. Then it must, so to speak, dump it into the lap of the general public and see what happens. The world would probably be much happier today if the aeroplane had never been invented, if ships had never been perfected that would sail under the sea or if all high explosives could be returned to their original elements and kept there "for the duration of the emergency."

But the human mind never did and never will permit itself to be so limited in its scope. If civilization chooses to use its bombers, submarines and high explosives to blot out civilization, the fault lies with our morals not with our brains. We must blame our statesmen, our theologians, our cultural leaders if they cannot keep the human within due bounds. Given national hatred, nations will fight. The club, the spear or the arrow in their own crude way can be very effective. So we maintain that we are quite justified in writing all we know about hypnotism.

Many an able critic might be inclined to add "and a great deal we don't know." Unfortunately there is enough truth in that statement to make it hurt, so to speak. We express rather dogmatic views on many points of hypnotism, views which we acknowledge cannot be substantiated by experimental evidence. We also point out, however, that proof is impossible in our present day society. We simply advance the problem and what seems to us a probable solution. To wait passively for scientific proof might be to wait another hundred years. If we can provoke our brother psychologists and the general public into demanding proof, even if we ourselves are in the long run proven completely wrong, we may have answers to some very important world problems in the next five or ten years.

That is one way in which we achieve progress. The extremist has his place in all science, psychology included. Be he a Freud, a Watson or a Pavlov he "starts something." The profession lines itself up in battle array, the pros and con spilling ink as generously as any military leader ever spilt human blood. When the smoke of battle clears up, the culprit has either been chased off the field or, most generally, both sides call an armistice, each agrees that the other was one-tenth right and nine-tenths wrong. Like most human wars no one appears to win much of anything. But in this battle of ink there is genuine progress toward truth, which is more than we can always say about other battles. And the extremist has his use in that he tends to get people in a fighting mood by the very dogmatism and novelty of his statements.

No matter what our bias we must admit that Watson and

Freud made, or perhaps provoked great contribution to be made to the science of psychology. We may thoroughly dislike the extreme behaviorist or the psychoanalyst, but in our more calm moments we can only regret the scarcity of this very annoying type of genius. The writer is rather amused at these last paragraphs. An extremist himself, he may appear to be claiming the label of genius as well, but he really has no delusions whatsoever along those lines.

We in America have been fortunate and unfortunate in this matter of hypnotism. The "professional" has really been of great service in one respect. He introduced the American public to hypnotism; but he instilled in that public a hearty distrust of the whole science. This was bad in that it carried over to medicine and barred its use by the doctor. But it had its compensations for it forced hypnotism to take refuge in the psychological laboratory. The average psychologist is not very much interested in the medical side of the subject. Consequently he began a thorough scientific investigation of all phases of the subject. As a result we in America have made more progress along these lines than have any other people. The book published by Hull in 1933 summarizes this progress, points out the woeful gaps in our knowledge and, incidentally completely overlooks one or two of the most important problems in the field.

Several problems seem now to have been answered to the satisfaction of the majority of psychologists. Hypnotism, it seems pretty well agreed is one form of exaggerated suggestibility and dissociation is probably a result of this. Moreover it is a form of "direct" or "prestige" suggestion which seems quite different from the indirect or non-prestige variety. This is a very important step because it ties hypnotism to other forms of suggestion, especially that of the mob leader.

Then it would seem that human hypnotism has no relation to animal hypnotism, another important decision. Even Pavlov fell into this trap, linking the human and the animal varieties, and making some serious mistakes in his treatment of the whole subject. Frankly we do not know very much about animal hypnotism but whatever it is it seems quite distinct from the human brand.

Then we seem to be fairly well agreed on another point. Hypnotism has nothing to do with sleep. This is very important as even Bernheim was in error on this particular point. The individual in the trance is, in all respects, just as much "awake" as if he were "normal." In fact, so close is the resemblance that it is quite impossible to tell the difference, especially if the subject has been coached to act normal. With this fact at the back of his mind the modern operator avoids many of the errors into which his predecessors very naturally fell. The "trance" we now know is not necessary in procurring any of the phenomena of hypnotism, at least if we mean by the trance somnambulism involving loss of consciousness. To be sure it helps but the work on "waking" hypnotism has established this point, even if it be more or less of only academic interest to the average reader.

As to these actual phenomena of hypnotism we seem to be in fairly general agreement. Where disagreement does exist it seems, to the writer at least, that it is largely a question of "operator attitude" a factor which seems of the greatest importance but which has been given much less attention than it deserves up to the present. The hypnotic subject co-operates in wonderful fashion and tends to give us the answers we want. This fact makes it impossible to apply the research methods of the physical sciences to hypnotism, in fact to many fields of psychology. The attitude of the experimenter means nothing to the working of a chemical formula, to the refraction of light or to a problem in higher mathematics. In hypnotism it is crucial and the writer would stress it as being the cause of much disagreement between very able operators.

We are fairly well agreed that, using suggestion in hypnotism as the touchstone, we can hallucinate any of the senses. Visions are present and convincing. It is easy to cause hallucinations in the sense of hearing, of smell, of tastes, of touch, in fact of any sense organ, including those of the internal organs. These are most easily obtained in somnambulism with its accompanying amnesia but, as before stated can be also provoked without loss of consciousness.

We would call the reader's attention to another very important fact which we gather from the science of statistics. The individual in deep somnambulism is still an individual. The ease with which we can get certain phenomena conforms to what we term the curve of normal distribution. This fact, it seems to the writer, has been overlooked in many investigations. The mere fact that the subject is a somnambulist guarantees nothing except that on the whole he is more suggestible than in the normal state. But how much more suggestible, or to what extent one can override his ethical background, is quite a different thing.

As a matter of fact, we would expect from this curve of normal distribution that a few subjects at one extreme would produce almost any phenomena, and a few at the other, even if somnambulists give us almost none. The great majority would fall in the middle. This means that it proves nothing if some one particular subject fails to give us the results we expect. Actually we would expect it, and would expect to obtain the more difficult and questionable results from only a comparatively few people even in the deepest trance.

Paralysis of limbs and contraction of muscles are easily obtained and on this issue there seems very little controversy. Such is also the case when we consider the question of automatic movements, provoked by suggestion. Rapport is also a well known phenomenon but there is now pretty general agreement that it is not genuine. The subject appears to listen only to the voice of the hypnotist but actually he hears everything. This is a little bit of acting, a pastime at which most hypnotic subjects are excellent.

There seems also to be little doubt but that we can obtain

both anaesthesia and analgesia, insensitivity to pain in the hypnotic trance. Our historical evidence would seem quite conclusive on this point, as well as present day research. There is just one little point of disagreement. Is it genuine anaesthesia or is it amnesia? In other words, there is a possibility that the subject suffers genuine pain in hypnosis but forgets about it on awakening. The writer can see very little evidence for this viewpoint but it exists.

We hear much talk of great muscular strength in hypnotism and here we find our authorities beginning to disagree. The writer strongly suspects this disagreement is due to operator attitude and is quite convinced that the subject in hypnotism may exert a degree of strength which is quite impossible under normal conditions. We draw this inference not only from the experimental literature on the subject but also from our evidence that the human can develop tremendous strength in other circumstances. This is clearly seen in the action of the drug metrazol where the patient may literally break his own bones in the violent convulsions which follow its administration.

Great acuity of the senses has also been claimed for subjects in hypnotism. Here the evidence is far from being conclusive. In fact the bulk of our experiments would tend to show that it does not exist. This also applies to those reports we have of a subject being able to judge time intervals with uncanny accuracy. We must bring in the verdict in both these cases of unproven but possible perhaps with certain subjects. We must have a great deal more evidence in this restricted field before we dare come to any definite conclusion.

We know definitely, it seems to the writer, that we can influence the activities of the autonomic nervous system, that part of our neural structure which controls the internal organs. It seems fairly well agreed that we can influence heart beat, especially if we use some hallucination to excite fear or anger in the subject. So also we can influence the actions of the digestive tract and of the sex organs. Beyond this point the evidence is very conflicting. Can we, for example, obtain blisters and skin bleeding by means of suggestion? Certainly not proven to the satisfaction of science and yet the production of bleeding would come under the action of the autonomic system. We see genuine examples of this in cases of stigmata reported in church history. This leads us to suspect that it would be possible, but would probably occur with only the very best subjects.

We should note also that there is no relation whatsoever between hypnotism and spiritism, at least in so far as hypnotism aids in producing such phenomena as talking with the dead, clairvoyance or telepathy. There is, however, a very close relationship between hypnotism and the mediumistic trance when this is genuine. Induced by autosuggestion, the trance is really a very fine example of self-hypnotism and gives us our introduction to those weird cases of multiple personality which are again produced by a form of autosuggestion, can be obtained by genuine hypnotism and can in turn be cured by the same means.

Psychologists would also agree that anything which we can obtain in hypnotism we can also get by means of the curious posthypnotic suggestion. This enables us to provoke the phenomenon at any future time, five minutes, five months, possibly five years. Frankly we do not know just how far into the future we can project these suggestions but we have some reason to believe that the time can almost be indefinite.

We also notice here some other very curious phenomena. By the combined use of hypnotic and posthypnotic suggestion we can get such control over the trance that it can be induced at a moment's notice and so subtly that even a good operator cannot note the change from the normal to the trance state. The fact of whether the subject is "awake" or "asleep" can be determined by certain tests, especially by his ability to resist pain. But without such tests the determination is almost impossible.

Another very interesting point not realized by the general public is that with this combination technique we can remove completely from the subject all knowledge of his ever having been hypnotized. We can bring him to the point where he will insist that he knows nothing about hypnotism whatsoever, that no one has ever attempted to hypnotize him and that he dislikes the whole subject. Yet the original operator or anyone designated by this operator can throw him into the trance in a second.

This leads up to a further point. The subject can also be rendered immune to hypnotism by any other operator except the one who does the hypnotic work or any other to whom he may care to transfer the rapport. This is very important when we consider the possible use of hypnotism in crime or in warfare. Owing to the peculiar situations existing in both these fields such control of the subject would be absolutely essential.

Any phenomena seen in hypnotism or the posthypnotic suggestion can also be obtained by means of autosuggestion. To be sure it is difficult but it can be done. The best way of initiating autosuggestion is through hypnotism itself. We use hypnotic and posthypnotic suggestion to give the subject control over himself. From then on he can provoke all the phenomena in himself but the writer regards this as a highly dangerous technique. The subject is liable to set up a condition of dissociation over which he cannot exercise proper control.

Finally, all the phenomena we see in hypnotism can also be found in everyday life, among people who verge every way from the normal to the actual insane. This is one reason why the study of hypnotism is so very important. We are able to duplicate the symptoms of neuroses and psychoses in our laboratory and to study them at our leisure.

We find many curious traditions about hypnotism which are either wholly or partly false. Literally anyone, even a victrola record can hypnotize. There is no need of will power, the hypnotic eye, or thought transference. It is all a matter of training and technique. To be sure, some people will become more expert at it than will others, but we see this in every walk of life, medicine, athletics, music or mechanical ability.

Nor has will power anything to do with the subject. The persistent myth that only the weak willed can be hypnotized is wholly a myth. As a matter of fact it is impossible to hypnotize the feeble-minded or certain groups of the insane because they do not have the necessary "will power" to co-operate. There is likewise no truth in another assumption, namely that women are more easy to hypnotize than are men. Nor are alcoholics or criminals. We do find that children between the ages of say eight to twelve are decidedly more suggestible than are adults.

It would seem that most of these traditions about hypnotism are false. Can an individual be hypnotized against his will? Certainly, for all practical purposes. He can at least be hypnotized without his consent even when he has declared he will never allow himself to be thrown into the trance. This we can accomplish by using a disguised technique which the subject does not recognize or, with a good subject, we can transform normal sleep into the hypnotic trance.

The dangers of hypnotism? Greatly exaggerated but quite definite. We are not trying to be humorous when we say there is, at present, far more danger to the operator than the subject. Almost any good doctor could become a good hypnotist and would certainly do much more good than harm. Yet, with the present status of public opinion his reputation and his income might suffer very severely as a result.

Again the tradition is wrong. There is almost never any trouble of awakening the subject from the trance, given a proper technique. The competent operator is far more worried over getting the subject hypnotized than getting him back to normal. Hypnotism properly used never weakened the will of a subject and it certainly never caused "fits," feeble-mindedness or insanity. The real danger with hypnotism is that the unskilled operator may leave his subject so suggestible that he is at the mercy of every one who, for whim or experiment, may choose to throw him into the trance. Also, that he may introduce conflicts into the subject's mind by forgetting to remove suggestions or posthypnotic suggestions which may run counter to the subject's ethical background.

There is undoubtedly some slight danger that hypnotism may be used for criminal ends. The danger is very small, however, when we consider the total picture. If the hypnotist were dealing with a subject who was already a criminal or who had definite criminal tendencies he could probably use this subject for his own purposes and probably conceal his part in the crime rather effectively. But should he attempt to use a subject who had no such character defect, he would have to be an operator of the greatest skill and would probably have to trick his subject into the crime.

This seems quite possible by removing from the subject all knowledge of his ever having been hypnotized and by rendering him immune to hypnotization by anyone else. The hypnotist would count on the subject's known willingness to co-operate with an operator in any type of foolish farce. Whether or not the subject would continue to protect the operator when faced with an actual trial, disgrace and imprisonment is quite another matter. The writer is inclined to think that, at least with certain subjects, the real criminal would go free. But, as we point out earlier in the book we cannot answer this question by any experiment so far devised. We would need the actual commission of a crime and a genuine trial. That is a procedure which is impossible in the psychological laboratory.

Similarly, we might very possibly be able to use hypnotism in the detection of crime, to uncover information which, at the present time, it is very difficult or impossible to get by ordinary means. But again we cannot answer this question in the laboratory. We must wait until such time as the police are willing to use this device and the general public to permit its use. Actually, once the public is educated to the real value of hypnotism we will find that the police will be glad to avail themselves of its use.

There is very probably a place for hypnotism in warfare, not only in its use by the intelligence department to obtain in various ways vital information for its own ends but also to protect itself against possible use of this device by others. It may be that the late war will answer many questions concerning use of hypnotic subjects for criminal ends because its use in warfare would be very close to its use in crime, both in the commission and the detection of crime. Needless to say, this phase of the subject is receiving intensive attention at the present moment and no one is in a position to say just what has happened or what is possible. That may make fascinating reading once the present international situation clears up.

There is undoubtedly great use for hypnotism in the field of medicine, but popular prejudice against it is so strong that the great majority of doctors simply dare not make use of hypnotism in their practice. This is a great loss because it was the medical man who first gave the subject respectability, who used it with great effect and who still does so in European countries where the stage "professional" has not turned the general public against it.

It would seem that hypnotism might have its greatest use in those mental troubles which the general public is inclined to regard as bad habits, in fact in that whole field of medicine we term mental hygiene. Also in the treatment of such other habits as alcoholism, excessive smoking, but not in the direct treatment of the narcotic drugs. Hypnotism has undoubted use in the cure of hysteria and hysterical symptoms. Also as a sedative, superior to any drug, but more difficult to administer and of use only with subjects in which we can induce at least a moderate degree of hypnotism, say one-third of all adults, practically all children over the age of eight years.

Our first step in making hypnotism available to the doctor is one of general education of the entire body politic. First we should prohibit the public exhibition of hypnotic subjects for purposes of entertainment, which we now see in our various theaters. This would remove the chief center of infection which has lead to the violent prejudice we have to the subject in the layman. Next we should educate him to realize that hypnotism is simply another branch of science which, like every other scientific discovery, may be put to bad use by the unscrupulous. The danger here, by the way, is far less than the danger we have from most other scientific inventions.

But the real problem in the use of hypnotism is not the control of its use by the psychologist or the stage performer, but rather a careful supervision of orator, press and radio. The psychological devices used by the great orator are practically identical with those used by the hypnotist. In fact we must learn to regard the orator and the mob leader as hypnotists, far more successful and infinitely more dangerous than any hypothetical scheming psychologist in his laboratory.

Hypnotism is simply exaggerated suggestibility. Whether this comes as a result of the hypnotic trance or by the emotions, the second great sensitizer of the brain, makes very little difference. Results are practically identical. The mob leader always has and always will make his appeal direct to the emotions of the mob in question. The more violent and less logical the appeal, the cruder the emotions in question, the greater will be his success. He knows the truth of that catch phrase, nothing succeeds like excess.

Science cannot lead, it cannot lie. It can do very little to make a basic emotional appeal. A chemical formula, a mathematical proposition, the hypothesis of an astronomer regarding the speed of light or the distance of stars, even the discovery of a new cure for pneumonia contain very little of the emotional element. They are or they are not facts and we leave it to the expert to decide. We can hardly imagine the Germans and the British in a great war because J. B. S. Haldane insisted that man was merely a machine while some great German claimed he had a soul.

Here we encounter a very ugly truth about this animal, *homo sapiens,* the one reasoning, thinking animal in all nature. We might term it the reality of unreality. A lie, once circulated, is with him potentially the truth. His high intelligence he uses only to satisfy himself in his insane pursuit of the pleasure principle and he turns out to be not a rational but a rationalizing animal. To the average German the scientific myth of Nordic superiority was grim reality, to his opponents even grimmer reality. The nonsense he circulated about the fiendish Jew was scientific nonsense if we wish, but terrible truth in so far as these unfortunate people were concerned wherever he crossed their path.

In fact, so far as human relations are concerned we may well ask the question of doubting Pilate, "What is truth?" Hitler may be a genius or a madman, as we wish. Fascism may be a plague or a model form of government, again we can take our choice. To the citizens of Warsaw, Amsterdam, Belgrade or London the question is purely academic. They have their answer, an answer which history has given us times without number but which we refuse to accept, namely that any ruthless leader appealing to the emotions of the mob can plunge this world into a welter of blood.

It would be well for us to center our attention on this form of hypnotism, for it is nothing else. Never before was it more dangerous. Radio and the controlled press are literally made to order for this type of leadership and when we talk of "making the world safe for democracy" we must realize that, psychologically speaking, the world was never more unsafe for democracy. Group hypnotism, mob leadership, call it what you will, was never more easy than in this day of syndicated press and national hookup. And democracy may find this new world an even more unhealthy place in which to survive than it has been for the last one hundred years.

We in America are cursed with the "holier-than-thou" attitude. It can't happen here. We must realize that it both can and will happen here unless we are eternally on guard. Somehow we must learn to recognize and discredit those leaders whose appeal is purely emotional, who are our real "professionals" in stage and hypnotic parlance. This will be an extremely difficult task, for all of us, no matter of what profession or trade, react largely on an emotional basis when dealing with our fellow human beings. The fact that we will indignantly protest the contrary merely makes matters worse, proving us not rational but rationalizing animals.

The problem facing us in this country is one of education. A realization that none of us has too much of the milk of human kindness in our veins, all of us are prejudiced, irrational, and that this has an emotional basis. If we can realize this for ourselves, and it is a very difficult viewpoint at which to arrive, it must make us more tolerant of the other chap when he airs his prejudices. And no dictator ever rose to power on a program of tolerance. The foundation of democracy, it will engulf the despot like quicksand.

The writer firmly believes that a certain mental attitude he is trying to impart will help greatly to preserve our present institutions. There is danger of a very real sort in hypnotism, but not where the reader has been taught to expect it. The highly emotional orator and mob leader is, from the psychologists' viewpoint, a much more effective hypnotist than any laboratory product. It is he who leads humanity by the nose into its bloody wars. We must learn to discount him, to refuse to be stampeded by his appeals to hatred and prejudice. We must listen always to that still small voice of reason and be tolerant in our own prejudices, for that is all most of our "convictions" amount to. If we as a people grasp this truth, America is safe for democracy.

INDEX

INDEX